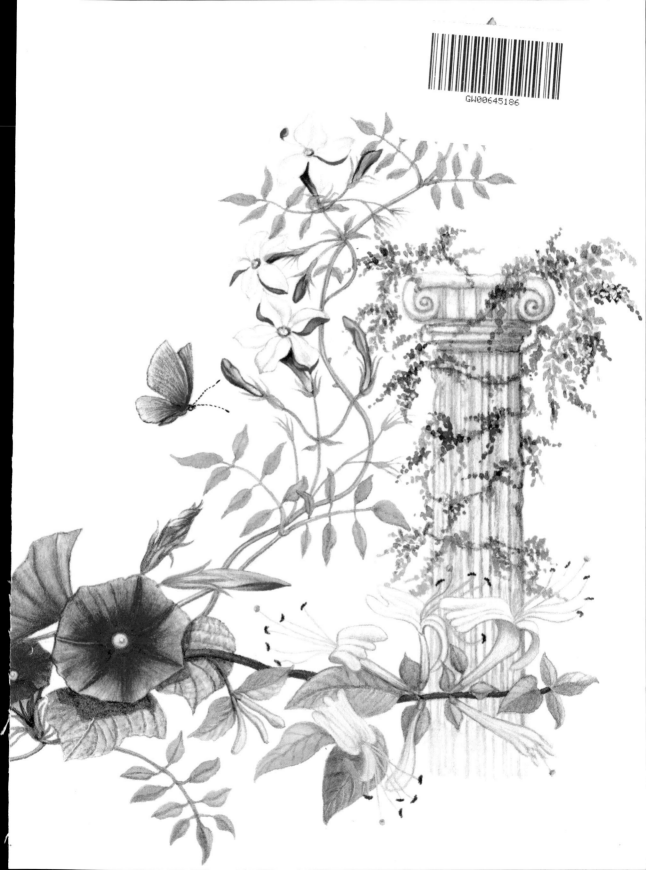

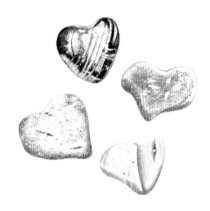

Published in 2021 by Unicorn,
an imprint of Unicorn Publishing Group
5 Newburgh Street
London
W1F 7RG
www.unicornpublishing.org

ISBN 978-1-913491-74-1

10 9 8 7 6 5 4 3 2 1

Designed by Felicity Price-Smith
Printed by Fine Tone Ltd

A Greek Island
Nature Diary

Jani Tully Chaplin

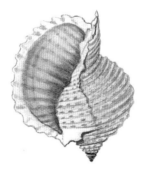

UNICORN

Look closely. The beautiful may be small.

Immanuel Kant

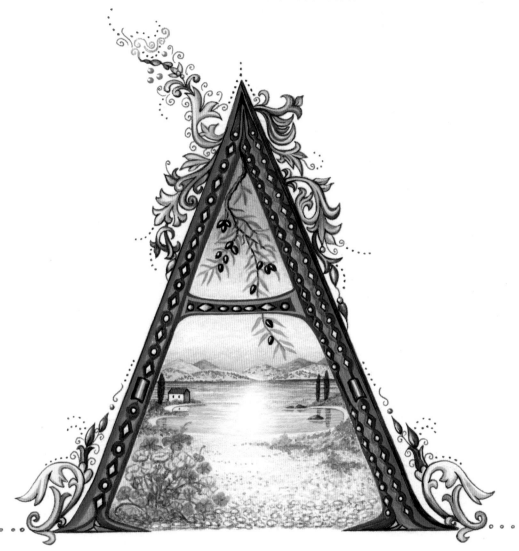

To see a world in a grain of sand,
And a heaven in a wild flower,
Hold infinity in the palm of your hand,
And eternity in an hour.

William Blake

This book is a very personal journal of watercolour paintings and pencil sketches of the flora, fauna and fascinating natural objects I have collected and drawn from life during the ten years my family and I spent in Corfu and the Ionian on board our catamaran, Sarava. Cameo scenes of the islands will perhaps lend a sense of place to past, present and future visitors.

The text briefly describes some of the therapeutic, olfactory, medicinal, practical and culinary uses of many of the plants, along with associated mythology and folklore. My favourite quotations and relevant lines of poetry, as well as some observations of my own, are scattered amongst the illustrations.

I hope those who read this book will in some way be infected with my love for the islands, their generous people and my passion for all things Greek.

Jani Tully Chaplin

Foreword by
John Seymour, Duke of Somerset

This sumptuously produced book captures the natural beauty of the Mediterranean island of Kerkyra. The Greek name for Corfu is derived from the nymph Korkira, who was abducted by Poseidon, god of the sea, and brought to this hitherto unnamed island.

This diary was written and illustrated by the author during the years she and her family lived amongst the islanders, exploring the farther Ionian in their catamaran. The accurately observed illustrations combine botanical, zoological and geographical interest into a most appealing format, letting the fascinating information about the many uses of the plants link up with the traditional poetry and prose she quotes.

This gives the reader a strong feel for the island's atmosphere. I defy anyone leafing through this colourful book not to want to flee to the warmth and history of Corfu that shines through on every page.

A Greek Island Nature Diary is a most unusual book that evokes the skills of an earlier, nineteenth-century writer, and will bring gentle enjoyment to every reader.

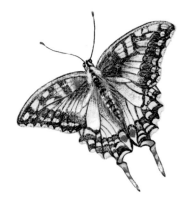

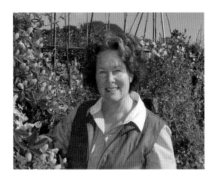

Lee Durrell at the organic farm, Jersey Zoo 2010 © Colin Stevenson

Durrell Wildlife Conservation Trust

is an international charity working to save species from extinction. Headquartered at Jersey Zoo in the Channel Islands, Durrell's vision is for a wilder, healthier and more colourful world. Established by the author and conservationist Gerald Durrell in 1959, the Trust's overall aim is for more diverse, beautiful and resilient natural landscapes in which species can thrive and people can enjoy a deeper connection with nature. Their approach concentrates on the rewilding of animals, the rewilding of ecosystems and the rewilding of people.

www.durrell.org

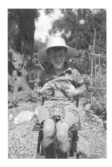 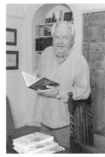 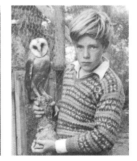

Photographs of Gerry as a boy in Corfu and in later life at Jersey Zoo reproduced by courtesy of the estate of Gerald Durrell.

The author contributes voluntarily to Durrell.

Introduction by Dr Lee Durrell MBE

To its many visitors, past and present, Corfu is an island paradise. It has attracted and nurtured painters, poets and writers, all inspired by the beauty of its coastlines and mountains, its olive groves and cypress forests and the warmth of its people. Nestled on the western flanks of Greece and Albania, it is also a crossroads for flora and fauna, where species from east and west, north and south, have mixed and mingled over the millennia. This plus its equitable climate and abundance of water have made Corfu one of the most species-rich and certainly the greenest of the Greek islands – a paradise for a naturalist.

My late husband, Gerald Durrell, brought the world's attention to this aspect of Corfu in his well-loved book *My Family and Other Animals*. He depicts his idyllic childhood in the 1930s, observing the wild creatures of the island – everything from earwigs to eagle owls – amidst the love and laughter of family and friends and endless summer days of sunshine and sea-bathing.

In this delightful book, Jani Tully Chaplin recreates the atmosphere of Gerry's childhood, no mean feat, as it is based on her sojourn on the island many decades later. Corfu was then experiencing the boom years of international tourism, which took their toll on the island's natural beauty, tranquillity and profusion of wildlife. And yet Jani sees through the disagreeable trappings of modern times with her enchanting illustrations and charming texts, which tell good stories as well as providing much fascinating information. She also, I am glad to say, pays close attention to the plants of Corfu, which are just as special as the animals!

As I write these words, I am sitting on the balcony of my old house in the middle of the island, overlooking a valley of cypress and olives and watching the aerial ballets of swallows. Behind me a swallow is sitting on a nest under the eaves, and in front of me a bronze-coloured wall lizard scuttles across the stone ledge. Now there's a flash of emerald green – a passing rose beetle, clearly on a mission to the tiers of multi-coloured wildflowers below. I am immersed in the magic of Corfu! Come and share the magic by reading Jani's book – it will bring you straight here!

Lee Durrell
Corfu, June 2020

Ελιά   # Olive   Olea europaea

In 1848 Edward Lear first visited Corfu. Soon after his arrival he wrote to his sister Ann: '*I wish I could give you an idea of the beauty of this island – it really is a paradise … The chief charm is the great variety of the scenery, and the extreme greenness of every place. Such magnificent groves of olives I never saw – they are gigantic.*'

Nearly two centuries later, the ancient, rampant and often unruly olive groves still dominate much of the hillsides and littoral, where their dense, shimmering canopy can reach as far as the tideline. Yet older islanders associate them only with toil, for every path that winds through the groves is still known as a *douleía*, meaning (path of) slavery; the word is separated only by accentuation from *douleiá*, the Greek for job or work. Each *douleía* was wide enough for a donkey, or more often a woman laden with yoke and baskets, to pass.

Fast growing and virtually indestructible, a growing number of neglected olive groves are more recently kept only for the wood they continually produce, much of it destined for the pizza ovens of Italy.

Mythology tells us that Athena and Poseidon were in a contest for dominion of Athens; Zeus agreed to award the city to the god who created the most valuable gift to mankind. Athena created the first olive tree on the Acropolis, while Poseidon created a horse. Athena's practical olive tree won her the city of Athens. To this day olive oil is occasionally used in lamps to light churches and homes, but its principal use other than culinary is in skincare products and soap in which its softening properties are highly effective.

Victors at many of the Olympic Games were crowned with olive wreaths, although laurel was preferred at Delphi; but my sympathy goes to the champions at the Nemean Games, where wreaths of celery were favoured.

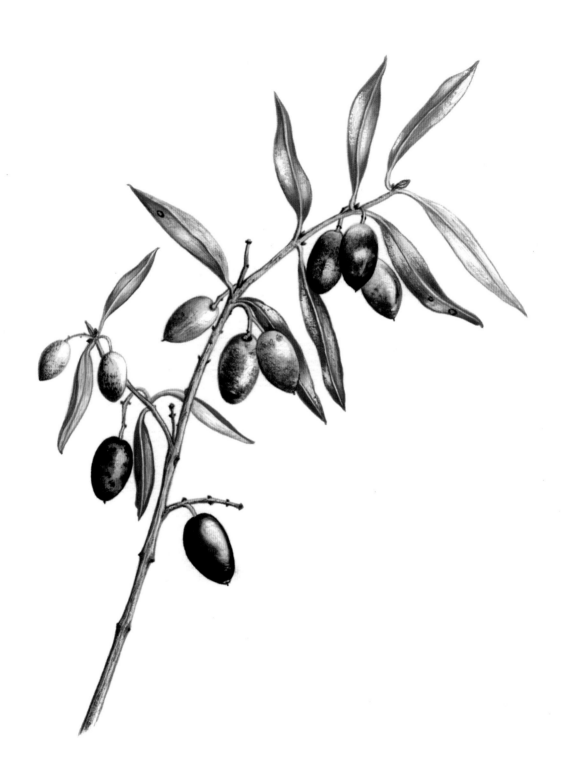

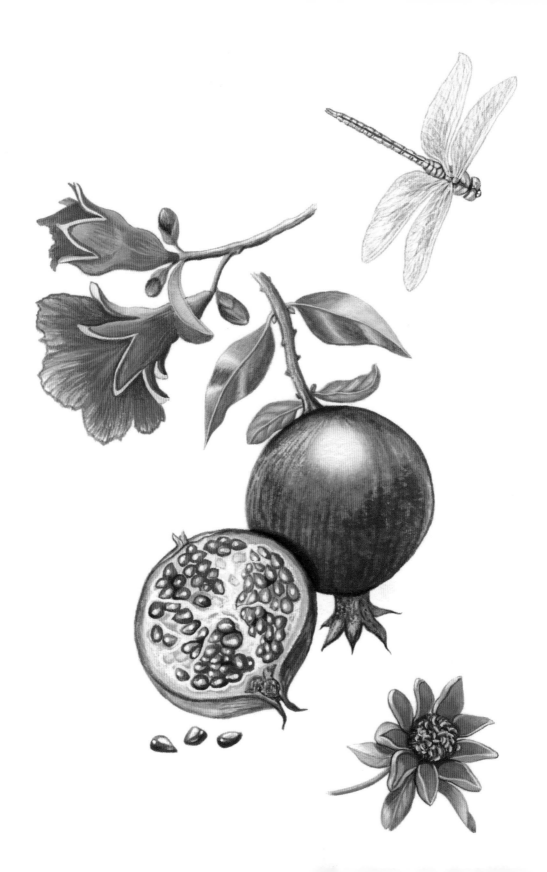

Pomegranate

Known in Greece as 'Aphrodite's Apple', the pomegranate was assigned to the goddess of love, who was reputedly born from the waves in Cyprus; there, as the myth holds, she planted the first pomegranate tree.

In Greek mythology, the pomegranate represents life, regeneration and marriage. When Persephone, goddess of spring, was taken to the underworld by Hades, she tied herself to him by eating a few pomegranate seeds – the pomegranate being a symbol of the indissolubility of marriage. The Thesmophoria festival honoured Persephone and her mother Demeter; it celebrated fertility in the home and on the land. In Rossetti's 1870 pre-Raphaelite painting *Prosperina*, Persephone can be seen holding a pomegranate.

This large shrub, often over five metres tall, has been cultivated since antiquity for the fruits it bears in such abundance; the seeds within the fleshy mesocarp are used to make sherbets, refreshing drinks and even ice cream, while the hard rind of the fruit produces tannin and a deep red dye. The juice is believed to reduce cholesterol, thin the blood, stimulate the immune system and to act as an aphrodisiac. Rich in fibre, fatty acids, vitamin E and magnesium, the seeds contain three times as many antioxidants as green tea or red wine. Children in Greece insert a straw into the ripe fruit and drink the juice.

From ancient times to the present day, a ripe pomegranate is cast onto the threshold of every Greek house at the stroke of midnight on New Year's Eve. As the fruit breaks open and the seeds are scattered, each seed is said to carry a wish for the health, happiness and prosperity of the family within. Similarly the first gift to a new home is often a ripe pomegranate, or even a young pomegranate shrub for the garden.

On a balmy August evening we dropped anchor in the gin-clear shallows beside the unspoilt east coast of Ereikoussa. The low dunes, largely untrodden, are home to the highly fragrant sea daffodil; as we had approached the shore, the powerful scent carried on the warm breeze from the island over the sea to us. Until I was able to identify them I called them sand lilies, as to me they resembled feathery petalled lilies growing in pure sand. I picked a flowering stem and swam back to our catamaran, holding it above the surface of the salt water, where, in the shade of the cockpit, I drew it as quickly as I could before the ephemeral blooms faded. As soon as I had placed the flower in a glass of mineral water, its perfume wafted around me as I worked on the painting, trying to capture the delicate beauty of its white petals.

Sadly the large lily-covered sand dune dividing the bay of St Spiridon from Antiniotissa lake in Corfu has been gradually eroded by storms and the footfall of tourism until it is little more than a small sandbank; only a handful of the plants have survived there. It is so eloquently described by Gerald Durrell in *My Family and Other Animals*:

> There was, however, a certain time of year when the lake was at its best, and that was the season of the lilies. The smooth curve of the dune that ran between the bay and the lake was the only place on the island where these sand lilies grew, strange, misshapen bulbs buried in the sand, that once a year sent up thick green leaves and white flowers above the surface so that the dune became a glacier of lilies...The curve of pearl-white sand was backed by the great lily-covered dune behind, a thousand white flowers in the sunshine like a multitude of ivory horns lifting their lips to the sky and producing, instead of music, a rich, heavy scent that was the distilled essence of summer, a warm sweetness that made you breathe deeply time and time again in an effort to retain it within you... the scent of the lilies came out over the water to greet us.

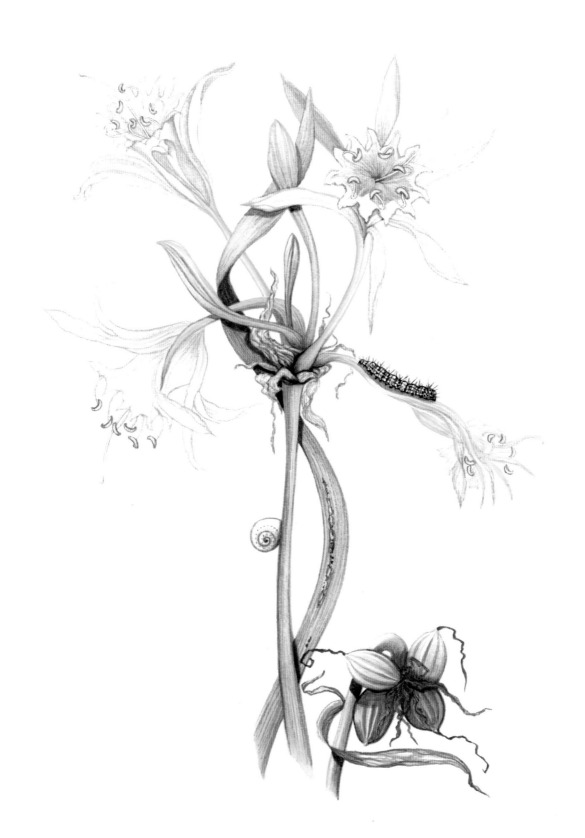

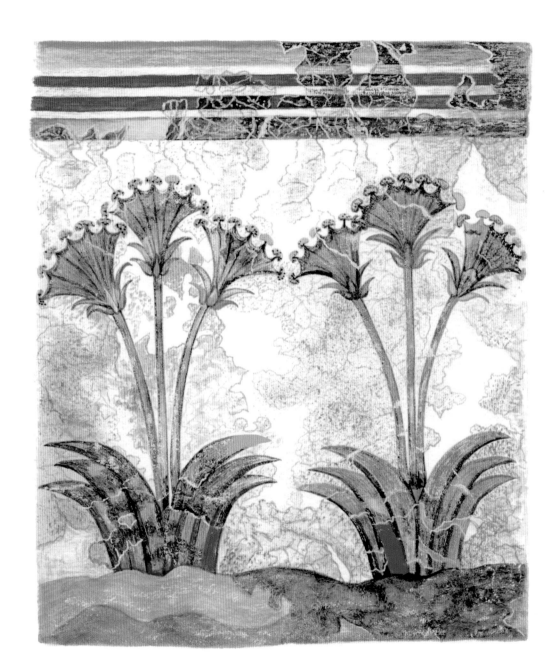

The lily, also known as *sea daffodil and lily of Knossos,* overwhelms the remoter dunes of many Greek islands from August to October. Although its habitats have begun to shrink, the lily is now protected by Greek and international legislation. The enormous green bulbs are often only partially covered by sand; some are the size of a child's football. Active in winter and dormant in summer, the bulbs store rain water during the winter months, which enables the plants to survive the hot, dry Mediterranean summers and thrive in nothing but sand. This hermaphrodite plant sheds shiny black seeds as the flowers die; the plants spread prolifically in the right environment.

The plant is pollinated by the convolvulus hawkmoth, *agrius convolvuli,* which, with a wingspan of 15cm, can only visit the flower in the lightest of airs. The tiny black seeds are carried away by wind and sea, transporting them to other distant beaches where they will bloom after five years and spread prolifically thereafter.

This rare and beautiful flower has been admired and valued since Minoan times; ancient wall and pottery decorations from the period are some of the world's oldest representations of man-made beauty. Derived from the Greek word *leiron,* white lilies were revered by the ancient Greeks, who believed they sprouted from the milk of Hera, queen of the gods. Lilies symbolise virtue and chastity, represent friendship and devotion, express sympathy, wealth and prosperity.

Sea daffodil extract has long been valued as an effective skin moisturiser; it also helps to inhibit the transference of melanin to the skin, preventing dark spots.

The impression opposite shows the fresco of sea lilies discovered at Akrotiri, Santorini, which was preserved by layers of ash and pumice after the devastating eruption circa 1600 BC. Standing nearly nine feet high, the original fresco is a tantalising glimpse into the extraordinary culture of the Minoan civilisation.

Αιγόκλημα   # Honeysuckle   Lonicera etrusca

Ithaca rose out of the early morning mist like a floating mirage. With the binoculars I identified numerous varieties of trees covering the slopes like a soft green eiderdown; olive, oak, eucalyptus, cypress, orange, lemon, pear and fig. Ashore I picked wild honeysuckle from a hedge on the quayside; its fragrance filled the boat. That evening at a harbourside taverna, eating swordfish caught that morning, we hoped it was not the one we had seen hunting as we sailed into Frikes harbour. The thick steaks, grilled over charcoal and accompanied by Greek salad and handmade chips, were delicious. Across a patch of water dotted with the tufty islets of the inland sea, the Greek mainland above Astakos shone briefly in the last glow of sunset, until pinpricks of light gradually appeared amongst the folds of the virtually empty, dark velvet mountains.

In Greek mythology the lovers Chloe and Daphnis could be together only as long as the honeysuckle was in flower. Daphnis asked Eros, the god of love, to make the honeysuckle bloom longer; according to legend this is why some species of honeysuckle remain in bloom as long as the weather stays warm. Honeysuckle remains a symbol of love in the language of flowers, representing fidelity. Its fragrance is supposed to induce dreams of passion.

Commonly called woodbine, honeysuckle is perhaps most famously mentioned by Oberon in Shakespeare's *A Midsummer Night's Dream*:

> *I know a bank where the wild thyme blows,*
> *Where oxlips and the nodding violet grows,*
> *Quite over-canopied with luscious woodbine,*
> *With sweet musk-roses and with eglantine:*
> *There sleeps Titania sometime of the night...*

In *Naturalis Historia* Pliny the Elder recommends a large spray of honeysuckle immersed in wine as a remedy for spleen ailments. In Greece the flower extract is used for treating bronchitis and asthma. A natural antibiotic, it is still used to treat many bacterial infections. Honeysuckle is pollinated at night by moths.

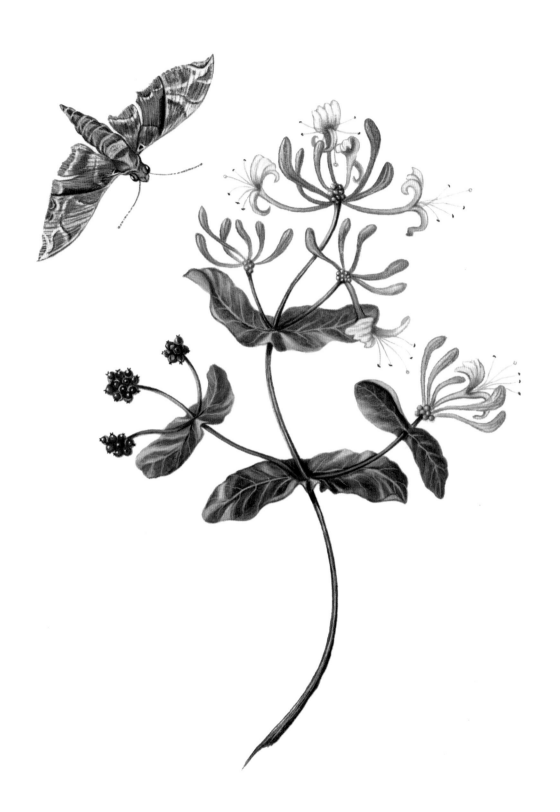

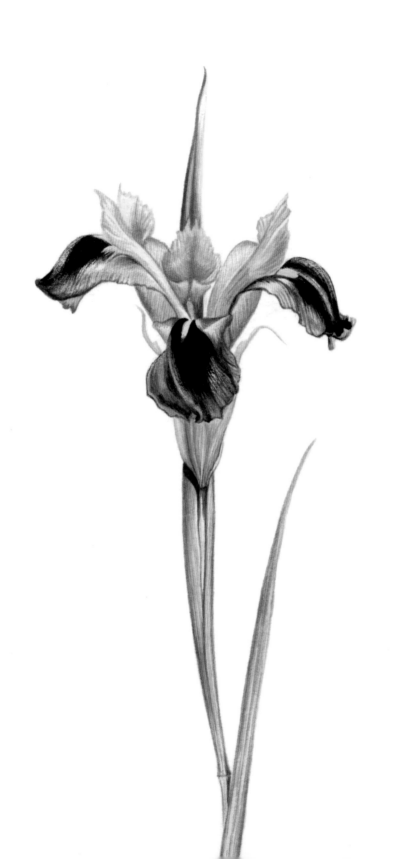

Snake's Head Iris

Hiding in the long grass under our ancient olive trees, a tall slim stem held an elegant flower which resembled a small iris. The three largest pale green petals were tipped with a velvety black which gave the impression of a fleur-de-lis. I was thrilled to find it had a delicate scent and was certain it must be a rare species, but as I looked more carefully I found several more. I soon identified them as snake's head iris.

The following week there were hundreds hiding in the undergrowth. Once in a vase of water their scent filled the house with a fragrance hard to describe; the closest I could come to anything I had smelt before was L'Air du Temps, a famous scent by Nina Ricci. Research told me this perfume has floral tones of gardenia, jasmine, sandalwood and – believe it or not – iris.

A sophisticated, elegant and intricately structured flower, it is sometimes called widow's iris and also velvet flower-de-luce, because of its resemblance to black velvet. The snake's head iris begins flowering as early as January in the Ionian; but even with a height of 30cm the flowers can be difficult for the untrained eye to spot, so well are they camouflaged amongst the long grasses and rolled olive nets.

Hermodactylus translates as the finger of Hermes; Iris, another heavenly messenger, was herself goddess of the rainbow. The iris genus was aptly named after the iridescence and colours of the rainbow; the modern Greek *ouránio tóxo* translates literally as heavenly bow.

Dioscorides, Greek author of *De Materia Medica* at the time of the Roman Emperor Nero, recorded that iris rhizomes – more usually flag iris – were widely used for medicinal purposes and in perfumery. Their roots retain a scent of violet long after they have been dried and the essential oil distilled from the rhizome is highly prized in the perfume industry.

Caper Plant

I have discovered some fascinating facts relating to this intriguing and beautiful plant. Hanging on the remoter sea cliffs of Corfu, seeming to grow straight out of the bare rock face, were fabulous trailing plants which resembled those of the tender variety found in the indoor plant sections of English garden centres. The first example I was able to study closely sprouted from the sheer side of an obliging rock formation, topped with a prickly pear, to which we had secured the stern lines of our boat. This caper plant fascinated me, looking so exotic and incongruous against the rockface. A multitude of emerald, heart-shaped leaves tumbled like green waterfalls towards the beach and sea below. In July delicate pale pink flowers adorned the plants, the shape of hibiscus blooms with a cluster of long white stamens, tipped with dark pink pollen, protruding from the middle of their petal trumpets.

Many people imagine it is the caper berry that is used as an ingredient in tapenade, the delicious sauce or dip made from black olives, anchovies, garlic, olive oil and capers. In fact it is the unopened flower buds that

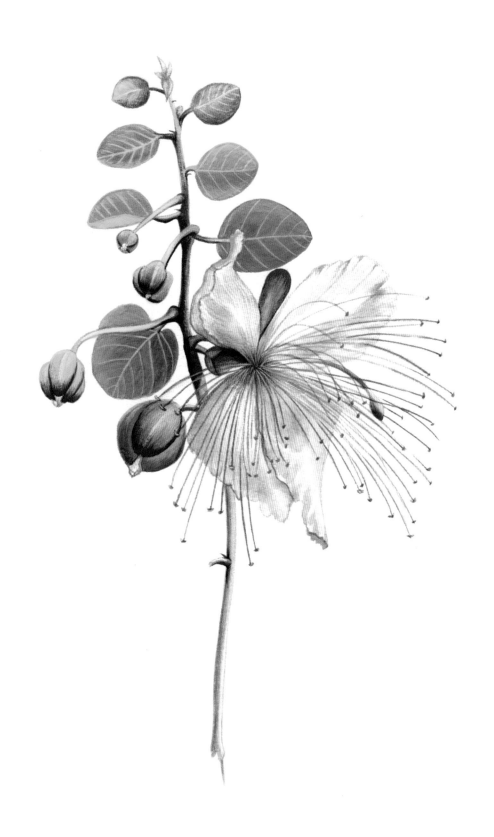

are pickled in vinegar and used in fish dishes, tartar sauce and Salade Niçoise, as well as for the paste itself; any unpicked buds will grow into the caper berry. Similar dishes were served by the ancient Greeks and used as an appetite enhancer by the Romans before banquets – not that they needed any help.

The Byzantines also served capers mixed with olive oil, honey and vinegar spread on slices of bread before meals, and in the Middle Ages an infusion of capers passed as an aphrodisiac. A speciality in Santorini is a dish made from the pickled young shoots of the caper and samphire pickled in brine which are served in a particular mezze dish called *Kapparofilla*. Tapenade derives from the Provençal word for caper, *tapeno*.

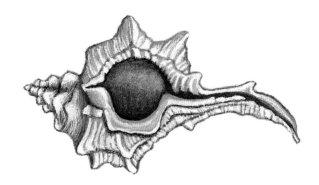

There was an old man whose remorse
Induced him to drink caper sauce,
For they said, 'If mixed up
With some cold claret-cup,
It will certainly soothe your remorse!'

One Hundred Nonsense Pictures and Rhymes
Edward Lear

As we pulled up the anchor, we noticed a tiny seahorse clinging to the chain. When we placed it back in the sea, it uncurled its tail and its body straightened completely as it dived down, like an arrow, into the Posidonia weed on the sea bed.

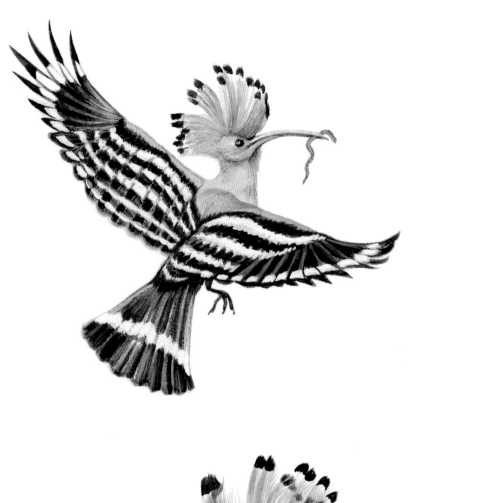
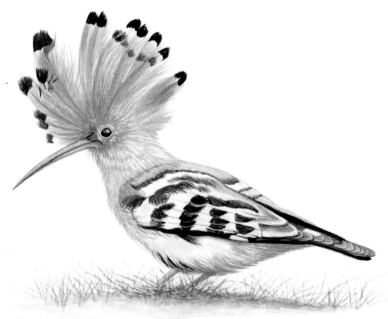

The hoopoe, comical King of the Birds in Aristophanes' *The Birds*, purported counsellor to King Solomon and, less flatteringly, the form into which Tereus was transformed in the gruesome myth of Procne and Philomela, is a welcome summer visitor to the Ionian. Nesting in the hollows of trees and walls, its distinctive call – often sung atop a flowering agave – is common at dawn.

I was fortunate enough to observe a pair of these delightful birds on a quiet path near the foreshore at Koyevinas, just south of Kassiopi; one kept watch from the highest branch of an olive tree while the other rooted amongst the dried grasses for insects. I had not come across a hoopoe since we lived in Spain, where they were quite common; indeed our finca, La Abubilla, was named after the bird.

The Latin name for this species, *upupa epops*, is a joy of onomatopoeia – hoop-oop-oop!

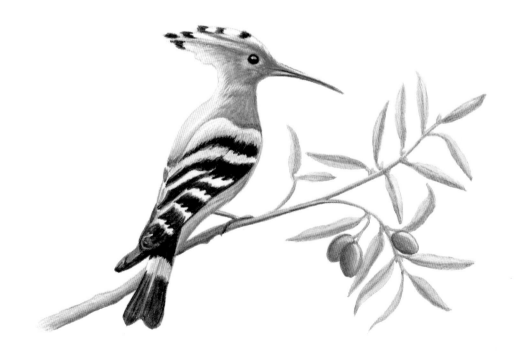

Shells

Beckoning me over to his boat, Andreas the fisherman tried to describe some objects he had found in his nets during his many years of fishing. They were small and round he explained, but he didn't know the name in Greek, let alone English. Were they pearls, I asked. They were not.

Back at his house Andreas produced two jars full of tiny, circular, shiny, flat, topaz-coloured objects. Tipping some into my hand I realised they were not shells, possessing no hollow interior to be home to even the smallest marine creature. I told Andreas I would research them in my natural history books. Eventually I found images of the objects; they were the opercula of *bolma rugosa*, a species of sea snail from the family *turbinidae*, 'turban snails'. When the snail dies, the opercula fall off.

Operculum is the name given to the plate or shield that acts as a 'door' to a certain type of sea snail's shell, serving as protection from predators and from physical and chemical stresses. When sealed into their shell sanctuary, the snails are safe in their impenetrable homes.

The cat's eye operculum is thought to offer powerful metaphysical gifts. Its spiritual properties as a portal to the ethereal realms derive from its physical properties, being a natural shield and protection from the elements. The natural Fibonacci spiral on one side, accompanied by the distinctive 'cat's eye' on the other, links them to the 'third eye'. Anyone working on opening their third eye may find this operculum to be a helpful guide; it could also be a great ally when working with water energy.

So closely connected to the sea by the number of opercula Andreas has collected and saved in his little jars, I expect his third eye is wide open by now. I must remember to ask him next time we are in Kassiopi.

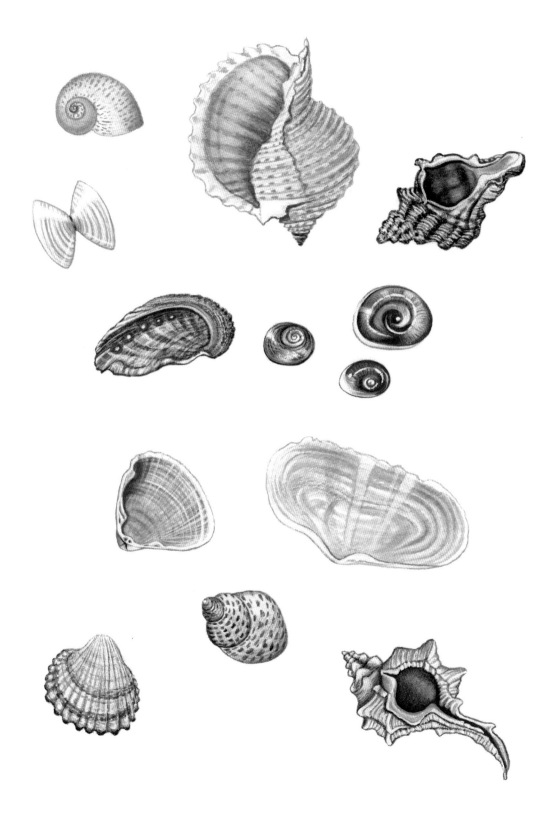

If love bore a fragrance,
it would be the scent of jasmine.

Jani Tully Chaplin

Γιασεμί

Jasmine

Jasminium polyanthum

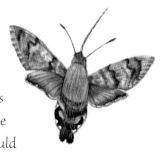

Growing like a rampant weed, covering balconies, railings, walls, anywhere it can climb, the scent of jasmine will always remind me of Greece and her islands. It is hard to capture the delicate snowy whiteness of any such flower; even the whitest paint looks cream as soon it dries on paper. The most accomplished watercolourists leave spaces on the paper where anything white, including highlights, should be, but I am not clever enough to do that.

So I use gouache, a water-based opaque paint with two shades of white in the palette. Unless one paints on coloured paper, any attempt to define white flowers on a white background results in the petals looking too heavily outlined. Not having much in the way of art materials on our catamaran at the time, I resorted to painting jasmine blossoms on a piece of rather crumpled brown paper saved from a parcel; it actually looks quite effective but the creases still show when printed.

From the olive family *oleaceae*, jasmine derives from the Persian for gift of God, which alludes to the intense fragrance of its star-like flowers. The precious essential oil used in aromatherapy acts as an anti-depressant, an aphrodisiac and as a fillip to self-esteem; those properties were well known to the ancient Greeks, who also used jasmine to treat insomnia and headaches.

Burned as incense in the religious ceremonies of many cultures, including the Greek Orthodox Church, its scent is widely found in modern perfumery.

Gloriously abundant in Greece, the jasmine flower symbolises elegance, grace, attachment, sensuality and modesty.

Mediterranean Poppy

During spring the freshly cultivated fields of many Greek islands are covered in blankets of bright red poppies of several varieties. Strolling amongst the blooms, filling my lungs with their hypnotic scent that is surprisingly strong in the heat, I picked a few flowers to paint later. I pressed some of the petals, as they only last a few hours in water, but over the years the colour has faded to a delicate shade of pink.

Greek mythology tells us that poppies sprouted from the blood of Adonis and were used as symbols of sleep and death. In ancient Greece, the flower was associated with the god of sleep, Hypnos, and with the god of dreams, Morpheus – whence the drug morphine.

More encouragingly it was also associated with abundant harvests; the goddess Demeter was often depicted with poppies and wheatsheaves in her hair, as in this eighteenth-century relief from Versailles which I have copied here.

The seed capsule and the seeds within were used by ancient Greek physicians as anaesthetic during operations; this must have been useful when Cleopatra purportedly underwent a nose reconstruction. More recently, poppy decoctions were used in Greece as sedatives for children.

Poppy seeds are widely used in cooking and baking. It is an ancient spice: poppy seed capsules have even been found in the remains of prehistoric lakeside dwellings in Switzerland. In traditional Greek mezedes, one of the famous 'little dishes' is *Saganaki*, pan-fried cheese; the cooked cheese triangles or rectangles are usually covered in poppy seeds.

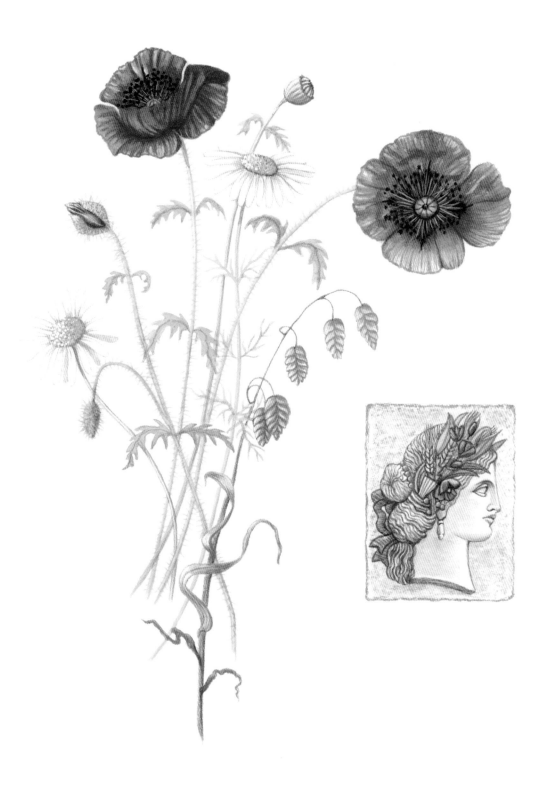

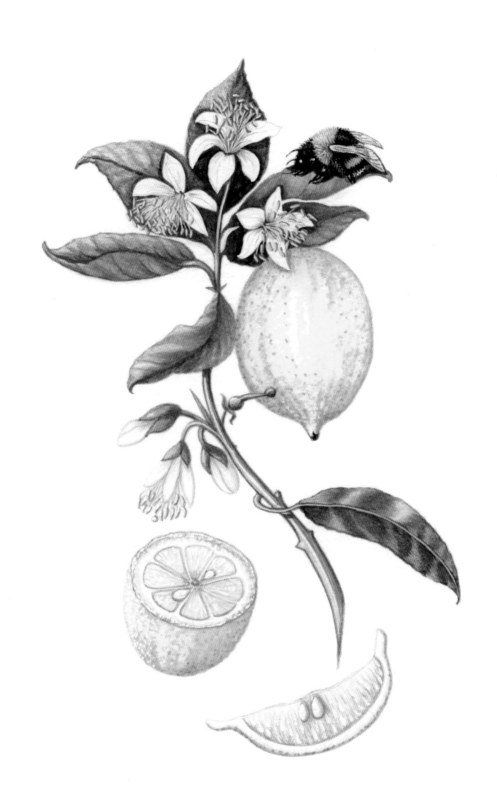

Lemon Tree

The sweet scent of lemon blossom pervades the Ionian Islands from November to early May. The trees grow to the edge of the sea, heavy with lemons larger and juicier than any I have come across; it always surprises me to see the waxy white blossoms sparkling amongst the glossy dark green leaves at the same time as the ripe yellow fruits. In Corfu the lemons litter the lanes, too plentiful to be harvested. Imagine my horror at seeing shabby cardboard boxes of tiny, shrivelled, overpriced lemons in a Greek supermarket chain labelled 'Produce of Argentina'.

Lemons have multiple uses, culinary, olfactory and medicinal. A swift remedy for a cough or sore throat was given to me by a Corfiot friend, who suggested adding the juice of one lemon to a glass containing a generous teaspoon of local honey melted in hot, but not boiling, water.

We had been at anchor off a remote islet when a guest developed a serious bout of food poisoning. Learning of our predicament, the kindly proprietor of a summertime fish shack quickly produced a plate of plain boiled white rice, doused liberally with lemon juice. Our friend valiantly finished the dish and immediately started to feel better; by the following morning the fever had left. My family employs the same remedy whenever a tummy bug threatens.

The juice of two lemons (or one Corfiot lemon) contains the daily requirement of vitamin C for an adult to maintain a healthy immune system. Limoncello is a favourite liqueur in Corfu, the recipe borrowed from southern Italy. More practically, lemon juice acts as a powerful eco-friendly cleaning agent, being both antibacterial and antiseptic; it also acts as a natural bleach. I regularly steep a slice of lemon in hot water in a cup or mug to remove stains from the china; equally copious quantities of lemon juice were traditionally used to bleach the teak decks on yachts.

Kingfisher

I nearly always saw kingfishers during my early morning swims; sometimes they would be perched on rocks or overhanging branches, looking for their breakfast. More often they would be skimming over the sea, their distinctive, piercing call echoing over the water. Surfacing for air unannounced, a kingfisher has more than once flown alarmingly close to me. On one sad occasion I was shocked to see a dead kingfisher hanging stiffly outside a bar in Sivota. Asking the proprietor why it was there, she said it was to ward off lightning strikes. I found this macabre superstition intriguing, so it prompted me to begin some research...

Medieval doctors and alchemists hung dried kingfishers in their treatment rooms, believing them to have magical properties, as did people who wanted to protect their households against lightning strikes or rather less dangerous attacks by hungry moths. English and French seafarers and fishermen would hang a stuffed or dried kingfisher, its wings stretched akimbo, from a string where it could freely rotate in the prevailing wind. Whichever direction the bill pointed would show the direction from where the wind would soon blow.

In Shakespeare's *King Lear*, the Earl of Kent asks: '*But how stands the wind? In what corner peers my halcyon's bill?*'

In Greek mythology, as in many other legends, the bird started life as a human being. Alcyone, daughter of the wind god Aelous, was inconsolable in her grief for Ceyx, her dead husband who had been lost at sea. The gods were full of compassion, turning the couple into kingfishers so they could remain together for eternity.

The scientific name for the common kingfisher, *alcedo atthis*, is *alcyon* in Greek, becoming 'Halcyon' by modern times. 'Halcyon Days' refer to the rare days of tranquillity when the Halcyon of legend nests on the sea for two weeks either

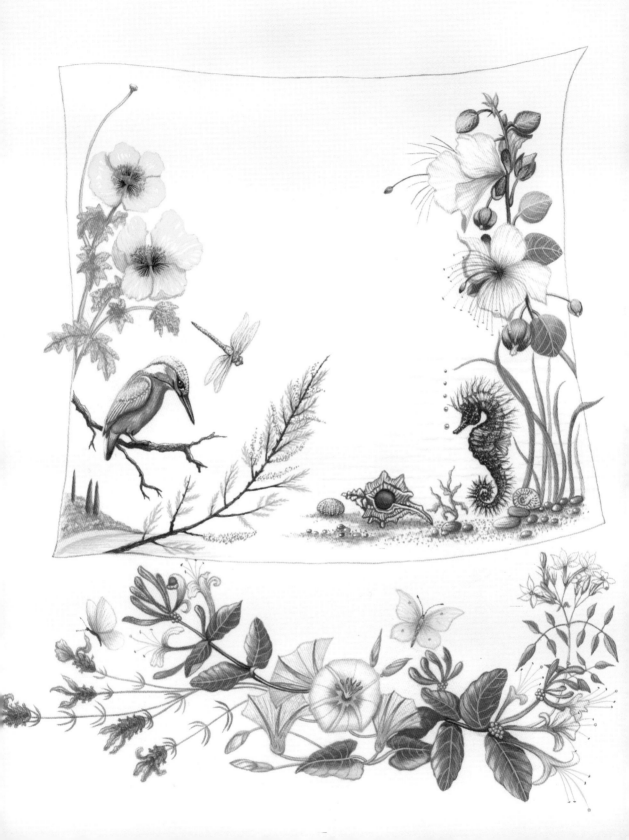

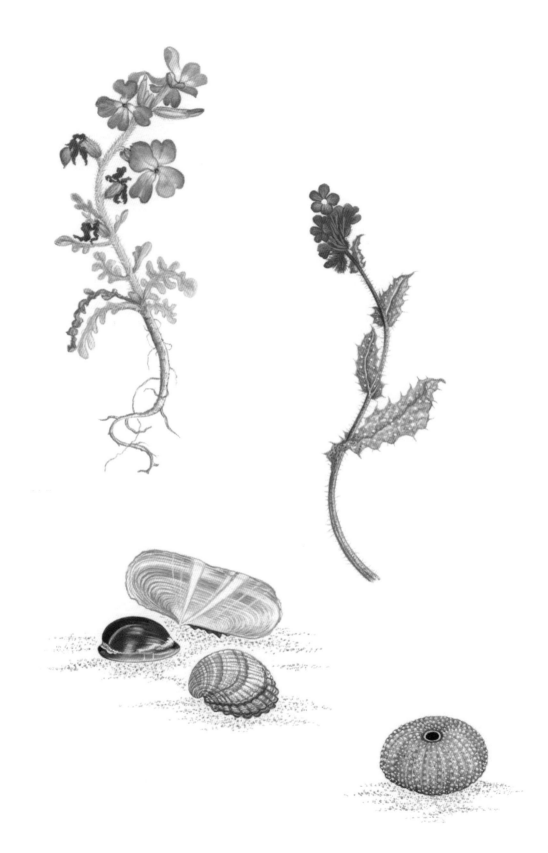

side of the winter solstice. With the ability to calm the waves, she keeps her floating nest (an intricate mesh of fish bones) safe while incubating her eggs.

The miniature, jewel-coloured oriental dwarf kingfisher, *ceyx erithaca*, is considered a bad omen by the Dusun tribal warriors of Borneo, its presence foretelling the coming monsoons. The sacred kingfisher of South East Asia is widely believed to have the ability to calm rough seas. In Australian aboriginal dreamtime stories, the kingfisher brought water to the land by means of underground springs; an area near Melbourne is called Ceres, possibly a derivation of *ceyx*, where Merri Creek is the ancestral breeding ground of the sacred kingfishers. The Wurundjeri people believed kingfishers carried away the spirits of the dead when the birds migrated back to Queensland each year. In Polynesian culture the kingfisher can control the oceans.

There seems to be a theme running from Medieval England to ancient Greece, the far reaches of Asia to the Antipodes, the remote islands of Madagascar and Polynesia to the tribal lands of Borneo. Surely some undeniable core of truth lies within such far flung and ancient cultures, who all believed the kingfisher had similar powers.

The common kingfisher is only hunted by a small falcon, the merlin; perhaps it is too fanciful to see a connection to the mercurial wizard of Arthurian legend. Did Merlin hang a dried kingfisher in his lofty tower at Camelot as an aid to his alchemy, or just to see which way the wind blew?

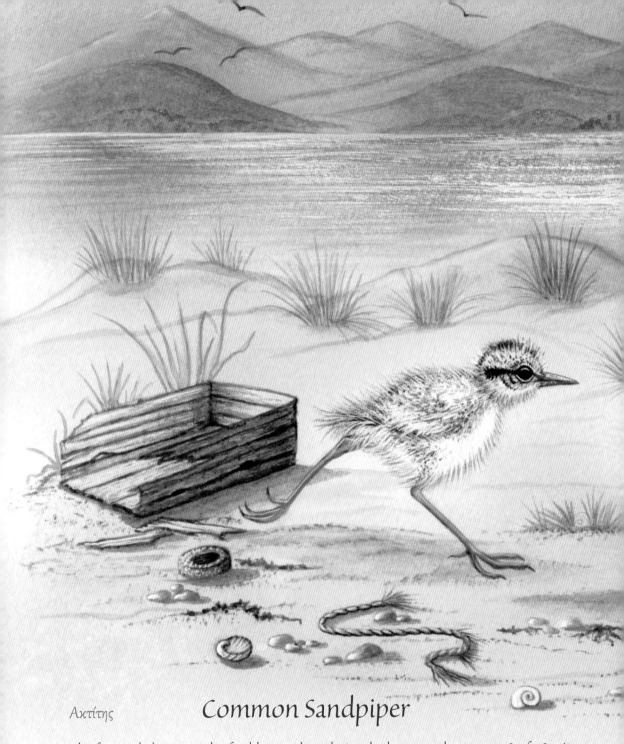

Αχτίτης

Common Sandpiper

The four-mile long stretch of golden sand at Almiros looks across the narrow Corfu Straits to the hills and mountains of Albania; they appeared close enough to reach out and touch on this May morning. We had the farther end of the beach entirely to ourselves and were astonished to see two fluffy sandpiper chicks. These adorable twins had been nesting in a

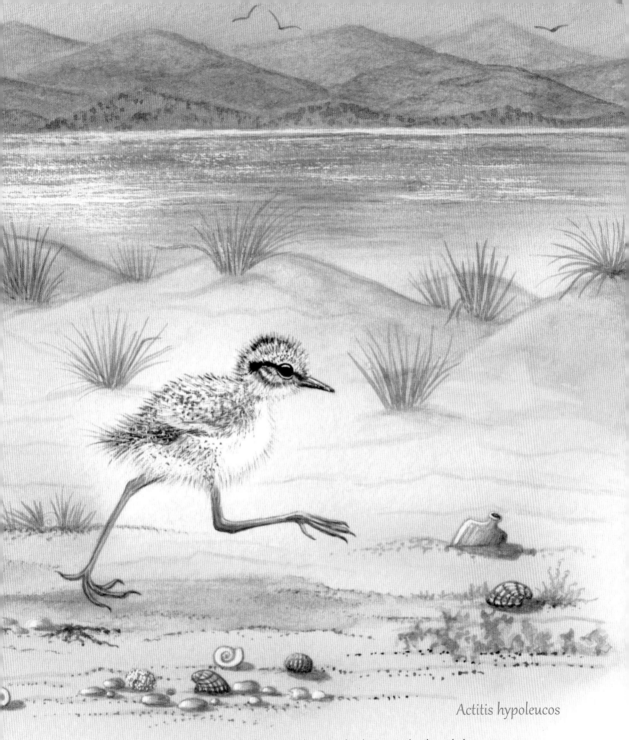

Actitis hypoleucos

broken wooden crate amongst the detritus thrown high onto the beach by winter storms.
As we disturbed them they ran on long spindly legs, taking great strides like little grey and
white powder puffs on stilts. We watched them, entranced, until they vanished amongst
clumps of sea holly, wild oregano and marjoram under a windswept tamarisk bush.

Papyrus

Wonders are many on earth, and the greatest of these
Is man, who rides the ocean and takes his way
Through the deeps, through wind-swept valleys of perilous seas
That surge and sway.

– Sophocles Antigone

From ten thousand years ago the brave sailors of the Cyclades used boats known as *Papyrella*, constructed from the buoyant stems of the papyrus plant. Some Greek fishermen were still using papyrus boats on lakes until the twentieth century.

I have found the feathery papyrus plants growing abundantly on many Greek islands, particularly around the Gouvia area of Corfu, the sheltered natural harbour where Venetian galleys were built and repaired.

Papyrus parchment is made from the sticky fibrous inner pith of the stem after the outer rind has been removed. The pith is cut into narrow strips, soaked in water and layered with overlapping edges, then hammered together to make a single sheet which is dried under heavy weights. When completely dry the sheets are smoothed and polished with either a seashell or stone.

Papyrus 'paper' was first made in Egypt in the fourth millennium BC. In Greek papyrus has a second name, *byblos*, used by Theophrastus when referring to the plant's uses in basket weaving and 'paper' for writing, as opposed to 'papyrus' when referring to its culinary use. The English word bibliography derives from *byblos*.

Some of the earliest forms of sandals and shoes were made from papyrus both in Greece and Egypt; preserved examples dating from 4,000 BC have been discovered.

Papyrus also has a fragrance that can be aromatic or woody, earthy and spicy. Although it is more popular in Indian perfumes, papyrus can still be enjoyed in some stunning contemporary scents such as the Atelier Cologne, 'Rose Anonyme'.

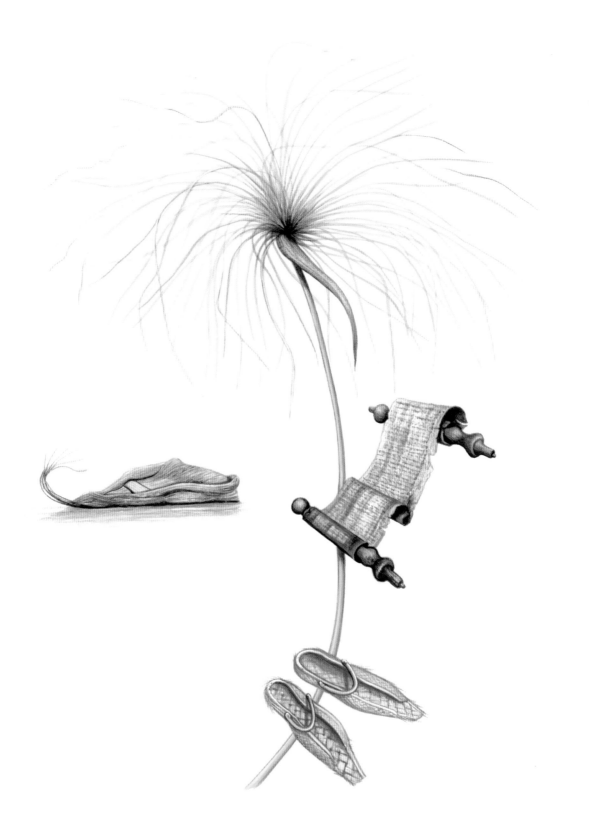

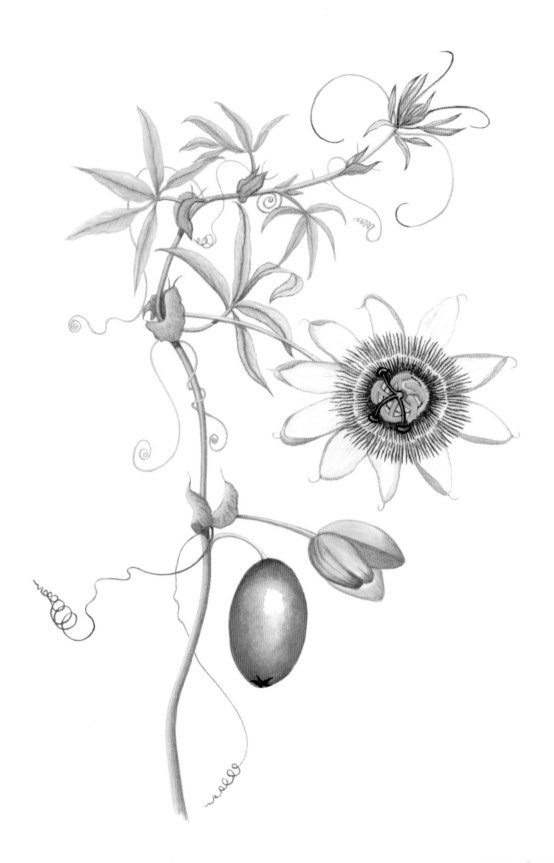

Passion Flower

Λουλούδι του πάθους   **Passion Flower**   *Passiflora caerulea*

The passion flower's common name derives from the description of its features as symbols of the Passion of Christ and the Crucifixion, rather than the human emotion. The tendrils are said to represent the whipping of Jesus; the flower column referencing the pillar of the scourging. The seventy-two filaments that encircle the head are said to be the Crown of Thorns and the top stigma symbolises the three nails. The five anthers represent the five wounds of Christ and the style is the vinegar-soaked sponge. The round fruit of the plant alludes to the world He was sent to save and the red stain from the plant symbolises the blood of Christ. The flower's fragrance is said to reference the spices prepared by the holy women.

In Greece the passion flower is called the clock flower, due to its twelve petals, and it was thought that the middle of the flower looked like the winding mechanism.

Popular in Greece for its calming and soothing properties, the plant contains benzoflavone which is proven to relieve stress and anxiety, as well as neuralgia and depression, insomnia and other neurogenic disorders. It is applied as a compress to relieve headaches. It is widely believed to improve the function of the respiratory system and is recommended in cases of asthma and bronchitis and in relieving menopausal symptoms.

Passion fruit juice can be used instead of lemon juice and the fruit is often added to fruit salads and pavlovas, cake icing and other desserts.

Snowdrop

Γάλανθος   Galanthus reginae-olgae

29th October: I saw the first snowdrops last night, on a corner of the lane from The Lion House to Eleourgia, gleaming like pearl-drop earrings in our headlights. It amazed and delighted me to see such early flowering snowdrops.

The ancient Greeks valued the snowdrop extract for its powerful mind-altering effects. In the *Odyssey*, Homer describes using the snowdrop to clear his mind of bewitchment by Circe: '*The root was black, while the flower was as white as milk; the gods call it Moly.*' This is the first evidence for the mind-affecting properties of the alkaloid galantamine, found in snowdrop bulbs.

Galantamine has only recently been used commercially, extracted from the snowdrop in the early 1950s when a Bulgarian pharmacologist noticed the inhabitants of a remote village rubbing their foreheads with the plants' leaves and bulbs. Naturally this led him to research this behaviour and develop the galantamine extract. In scientific terms, galantamine is a reversible, competitive acetylcholine – a chemical of great importance in brain function. Galantamine was officially approved as a drug in Bulgaria in 1958 and in the USA in 2001.

It remains a mystery how the Bulgarian villagers knew about the power of the snowdrop plant. Could the knowledge have been passed down from the ancient Greeks? Since the Medieval ages, Byzantine Greeks and the Southern Slavs have had a close relationship; Orthodox Christianity was brought to Bulgaria and the rest of the Balkans by the Byzantine Empire.

Nowadays galantamine has been approved for use in the management of Alzheimer's disease and mild dementia in over seventy countries worldwide, including Great Britain.

So many priceless remedies have been lost in the mists of time, but thanks to the popularity of homeopathy it is possible to revisit the expertise of the ancient Greeks. In my opinion we should never dismiss traditional remedies as 'old wives' tales'; the old wives knew a thing or two!

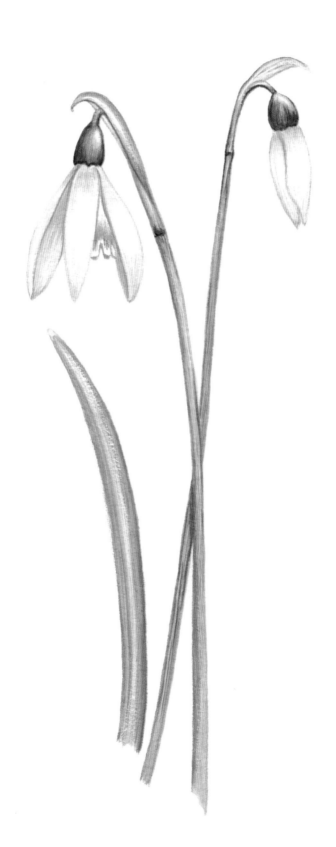

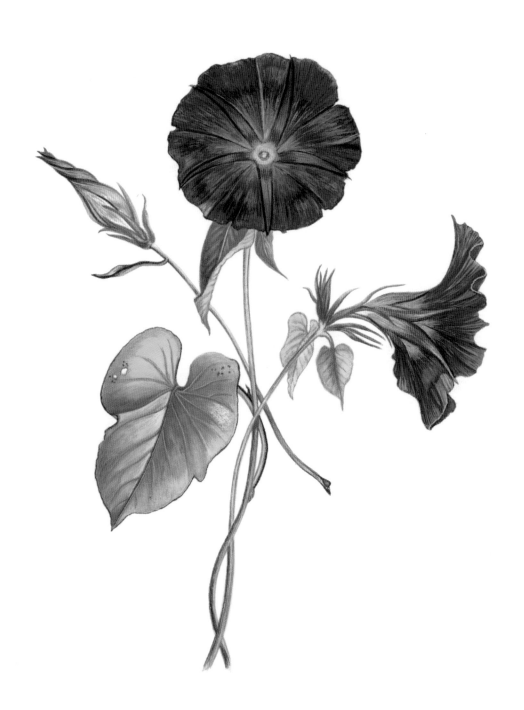

Convolvulus
Morning Glory

I saw the most stunning example of convolvulus in one of the neatest tourist harboursides in the Ionian Islands, Fiskardo in Kefalonia where our catamaran was moored on the quay for the first of many visits. Walking a few yards uphill I was dazzled by rampant morning glory plants climbing on railings and stone walls. The plants were humming with pollinating insects on the impressive trumpet flowers, their indigo blooms replicating the deeper sea beyond the moored yachts.

Near the Nautical and Environmental Museum was a whole hedge of intertwining morning glory and jasmine, their colours perfectly complementing each other, the scent of jasmine filling the balmy evening air. As we sailed down the west coast of Lefkas that morning, two pilot whales had crossed our bows less than a hundred yards in front. They swam leisurely on the surface for several minutes, turning to keep pace with us before disappearing from view. The museum has the skeleton of a pilot whale, beside which visitors were asked to log sightings in a record book as an aid to studies of marine life in the area.

In Corfu I sketched a battered, rusty and long dead truck lying on its chassis in the undergrowth by the roadside, completely smothered by *convolvulus ipomoea purpurea* – its electric blue flowers literally glowing in the morning sun.

Ipomoea has a dual meaning in the language of flowers – love or mortality.

Escaped from cultivation, the plant has become naturalised in Greece and her islands and most of the Mediterranean. Traditionally it is grown as fencing to contain livestock and other animals in the north western Himalayas.

The seeds have diuretic and laxative properties and are used in treatments accordingly. Containing small quantities of the hallucinogen LSD, the seeds have also been used in the treatment of some mental disorders.

Καλαμίνθη   # Calamint   Clinopodium nepeta

I made a fascinating discovery one humid autumn evening while walking under the olive trees on our land. A mosquito landed on my arm and as I swatted it I could feel the sting itching before the dead insect had reached the ground; a lump was forming so I quickly looked for something to soothe it. I have detested mosquitoes ever since a long summer spent in Thailand as a teenager, blissfully unaware that July and August were the start of the rainy season when mosquitoes began breeding in every klong, lake and puddle ; I had returned to England looking as if I had smallpox.

Knowing thyme was a natural antiseptic, I picked a sprig and rubbed it vigorously on the sting. Within seconds the itching had completely subsided and the swelling started to reduce. The remnants of the plant in my hand didn't smell like thyme but had a pleasantly pungent smell reminiscent of camphor, mint and something else I couldn't quite place.

I picked a bunch to take back to the boat to see if I could identify it from my copy of *Mediterranean Plants*. The plant was *Clinopodium nepeta*, known as lesser calamint, a perennial herb of the mint family. The tiny green leaves and the even tinier lilac-blue flowers of the plant looked so insignificant that it was hard to believe it was so powerful against mosquito bites.

After more research I discovered that this little plant, well known and highly valued by ancient and modern Greeks alike, was always planted close to their houses to ward off mosquitoes and snakes.The leaves have a high menthol content and were used by ancient Greeks as an antidote to snake bites. Delving deeper into its history, I was astonished to read that in Greek Mythology, calamint was the only plant believed to repel the legendary gargantuan Basilisk.

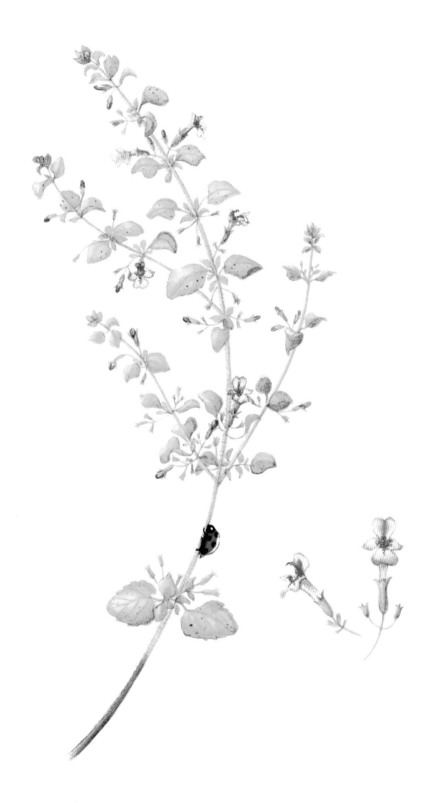

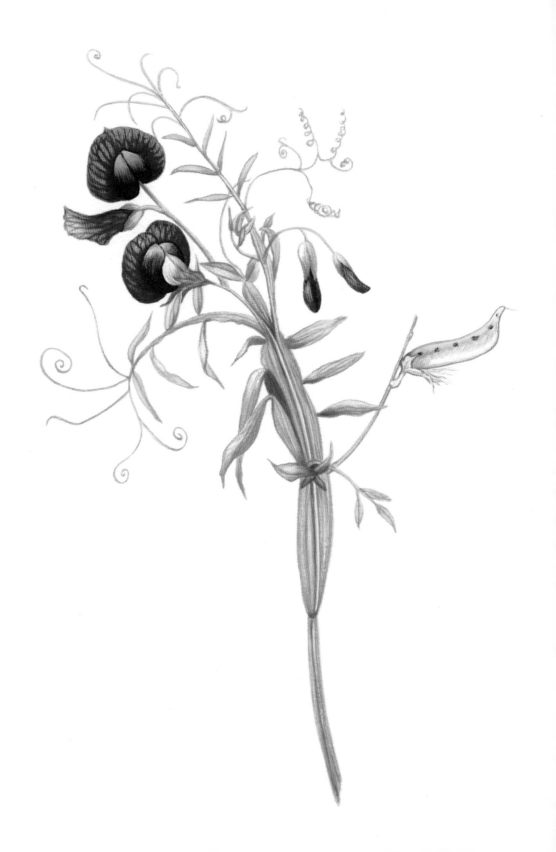

Λάθυρος   Wild Pea   Lathyrus clymenum

The Greek name is *lathyros*; the prefix – *la* – translates as 'very' and the suffix – *thyros* – means 'passionate'. *Clymenum* has a less attractive meaning, coming from the Latin *Clymenus*, meaning 'Scorpion's Tail', which can only refer to the curling tendrils with which the plant is able to climb. Native to the Mediterranean and cultivated on the island of Santorini, the seeds are used in a dish called *fava santorinis*.

The people of Santorini and neighbouring Greek islands have been cultivating this species for over 3,500 years. Frequent volcanic explosions on Santorini provided a peculiar ecosystem – the unique mixture of volcanic ash, cellular soil and humidity from the sea suits the plant and has made its bean invaluable as a food crop.

The fava, or beans, are boiled and then mixed into a purée, similar to hummus. With a very high protein content, it is usually served with chopped onion, olive oil and lemon juice. There is evidence that pulses, particularly wild lentils, were cultivated in Greece in 6,000 BC. The Greek microclimate has been ideal for the evolution of such crops, providing a highly nutritional but low-cost food source, helping the Greek people to survive famines and wars throughout their history.

Men and women who ate peas continuously became impotent upon the legs. – Hippocrates

Hippocrates was referring to Lathyrism, a condition which can cause paralysis of the legs, resulting from eating raw peas from the *lathyrus* variety. The seeds contain a substance which can damage the nerves of both humans and domestic animals if eaten in quantity over several months. The ancient Greeks were the first to recognise Lathyrism; associated with famine, the disease last occurred in Greece during the Second World War.

The peas can only be eaten raw in very small quantities; the toxin is destroyed by heat if the beans are first soaked overnight and well cooked.

Ταμίας   # European Chipmunk   *Eutamias sibiricus*

During one autumn visit to Old Perithia I found an empty walnut shell which had been nibbled by a chipmunk. We had first seen these little charmers when viewing a converted but dilapidated olive press near Liapades. The traditional wood panelled ceiling was painted white; as we were admiring it, something scuttled out of a very convenient hole in one of the panels. The tiny creature looked rather like a squirrel, but its striped markings distinguished it as a chipmunk. It froze, looking down at us, not in the least worried by our presence; it almost looked as if it was annoyed that we were there at all. It chittered in a way that said: 'Go away, this is my house!', as a second identical chipmunk, perhaps the inquisitive wife, popped out of the hole. They watched us for several minutes and I'm sure I could see them frowning as we left them in peace to scamper around the ceiling.

Siberian chipmunks normally grow to 50–150g; this species is relatively small compared to other *sciuridae* (the squirrel family). Siberian chipmunks were only found in their native eastern Asia until the 1960s, when the species was introduced to European countries. In the 1960s, South Korea exported these animals to Europe as part of the pet trade. Between 1960 and 1980, South Korea exported more than 200,000 chipmunks to Europe.

By the 1970s, the Siberian chipmunk inhabited suburban forests and urban parks in most European countries. This was mostly caused by owners releasing the animals because they no longer wanted them as pets, or freeing the chipmunks on purpose to live naturally in the wild. Other Siberian chipmunks escaped from captivity and inhabited the forests of Europe. Dutch chipmunks are escapees from a former zoo in Tilburg; when the zoo was shut down and the other animals moved away, many chipmunks were left behind in their underground residences.

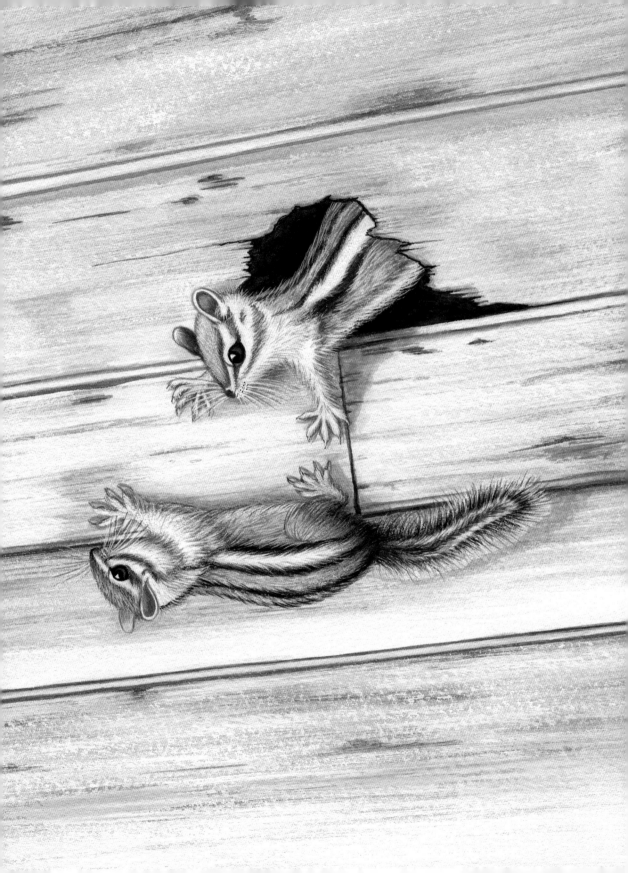

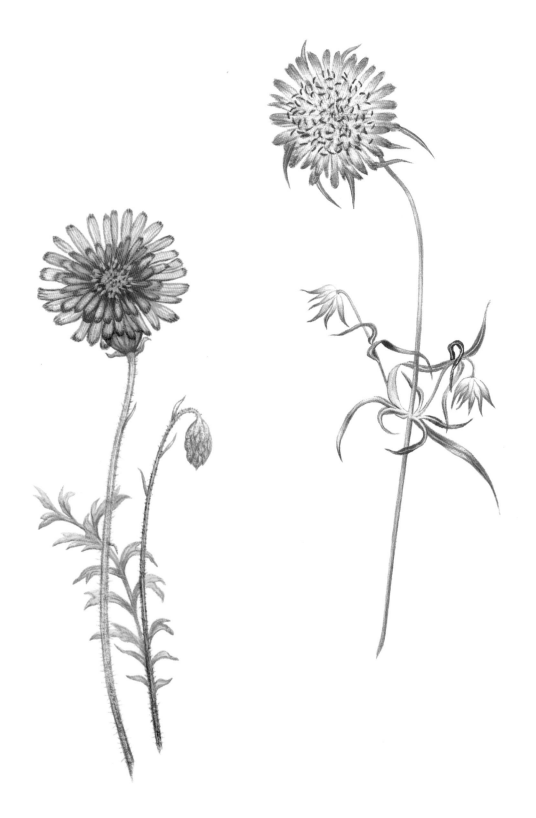

Cyclamen

The soft damp ground in the olive groves, shaded by the venerable trees, is bedecked in spring and autumn with the pale pink flowers of cyclamen. Their delicate flowers and heart-shaped leaves bring joy to all who see them. Strolling along some of the pebble beaches, I even found them growing by the foreshore wherever there were trees to provide shade.

Gerald Durrell describes them beautifully in *My Family and Other Animals*:

> *I called these three little groves the Cyclamen Woods, for in the right season the ground beneath the olive-trees was flushed magenta and wine red with the flowers of cyclamen that seemed to grow more thickly and more luxuriantly here than anywhere else in the countryside. Their flashy, circular bulbs, with their flaky peeling skin, grew in beds like oysters, each with its cluster of deep green, white-veined leaves, a fountain of beautiful flowers that looked as though they had been made from magenta-stained snowflakes.*

Purely for the sake of study and to paint the plant, I carefully lifted a protruding tuber from the top of an ancient low stone wall behind the beach at Kalami in north east Corfu where the plants grew abundantly. The tubers are extraordinarily large, rather like a dark brown potato but almost circular in shape. The leaves and flowers grow directly out of the rough skin, on the topside of the tuber. I brought my treasured specimen, wrapped in a damp cloth, back to England in the car; it flowers happily twice each year in a sheltered spot in my garden in north Cornwall.

Nuts and Seeds

With the first autumn nip in the air, the familiar Greek island summer scents of sun creams, kebabs and flowers are replaced overnight with those of roasting chestnuts, casseroles and wood smoke. In Corfu Town the street vendors replace the fruit and flowers they sold in the spring and summer with sweet chestnuts and corn on the cob, roasting them over little portable charcoal braziers; the tantalising aroma drifting in the cool air makes it impossible to pass by without buying some. The hot chestnuts are sold in small paper cones which have the added advantage of warming the hands on a chilly day.

The image of the Greek chestnut seller has inspired painters, poets, authors and song writers. Every other open-backed truck trundling along the roads on their way to market would be overflowing with chestnuts or walnuts, freshly picked from the high hill villages of the island.

Alexander the Great planted chestnut trees wherever he went. Chestnut festivals are held in autumn each year on many of the Greek islands. The picturesque mountain village of Agiasos on the northern Aegean island of Lesbos is famous for its chestnut forest and the annual Chestnut Feast held in November is to welcome the new harvest.

Chestnuts have a high nutritional value; chestnut spread is a Greek delicacy and used in 'spoon sweets' and confectionery.

Resistant to warping, chestnut wood was traditionally used for flooring in Corfu; examples can still be seen in some of the older mansions on the island.

On the Aegean island of Kea, where thousands of trees make up the ancient oak forest, acorns are undergoing a revival as a staple of the local culinary life and are benefitting the economy of the island. Acorns are similarly nutritious and have sustained entire Greek populations and armies over the millennia.

The Greek expression to 'pull someone's chestnuts out of the fire' suggests boldness and bravery.

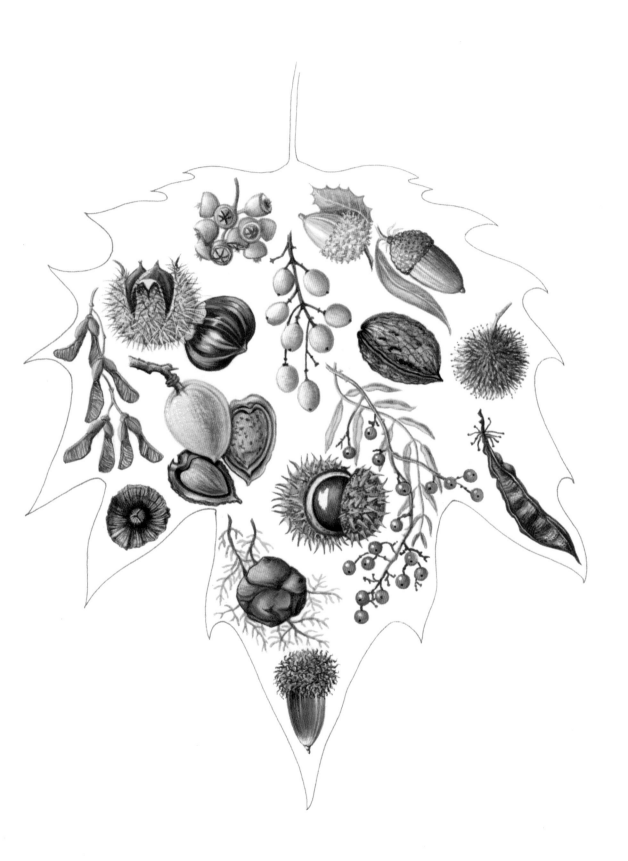

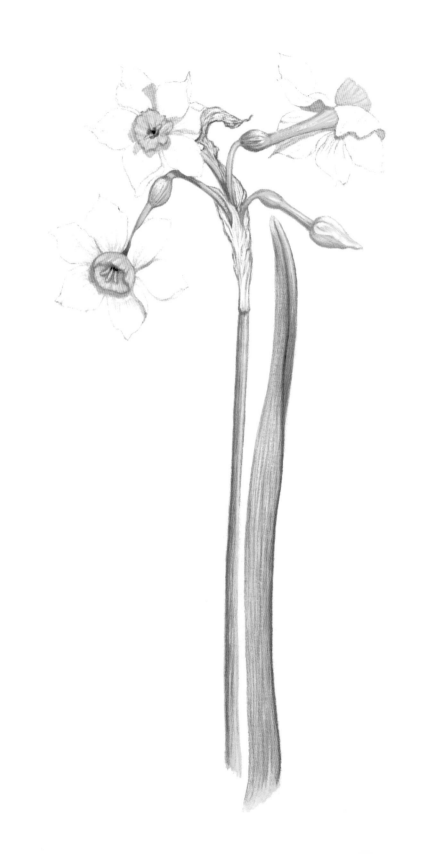

Narcissus

For two weeks I had kept an enormous bunch of sweetly scented narcissus in water, hoping they would last until Christmas Day. I had found them growing wild on the clifftops above a pebble beach near Kassiopi and picked about thirty-six stems; I say I picked them, but in fact it was Jeremy who had risked life and limb to hang over the edge of the precipice to gather them for me. On Christmas Day I placed them in the middle of the dining table and their exotic perfume filled the room.

In Greek mythology Narcissus, distinguished for his beauty, was the son of the river god Cephissus and the nymph Liriope. According to Ovid's *Metamorphoses*, Liriope was told by the blind seer, Tiresias, that Narcissus would have a long life as long as he never recognised himself; however he fell in love with his own reflection in the waters of a spring and died, the flower that bears his name springing up on the very same spot. The Greek traveller and geographer Pausanias, in *Description of Greece*, said it was more likely that Narcissus, to console himself for the death of his beloved twin sister, his exact counterpart, sat gazing into the spring to recall her features.

The botanical name 'daffodil' only dates back to the 1500s, prior to which time these flowers were called 'affodyle', meaning 'that which comes early' in old English. The plants contain a variety of protective alkaline compounds which can be poisonous. although many of these alkaloids have therapeutic applications and have been used in traditional medicine for thousands of years.

The Alzheimer's drug Galantamine is derived from alkaloid extracts found in several species of Narcissi and is still widely used today. Narciclasine, an isolate, taken from daffodil bulbs has been the ongoing focus of several new medical studies; initial results suggest it could be effective in the treatment of breast cancer.

Μαστίχα   # Mastic Tree   Pistacia lentiscus

A common part of Greek maquis, the mastic is usually seen as a low evergreen bush, although it can grow into a substantial tree. The plant, which favours dry and stony ground, smells acridly resinous and an incision on the bark will bring a flow of mastic resin. When dried, the resin is collected and has been harvested since the time of ancient Greece and used as a medicine, a varnish and a chewing gum to clean teeth and freshen the breath. I find it rather amusing to imagine the great philosophers and playwrights of ancient Athens chewing gum as they worked.

Containing antioxidants, said to support the plant's therapeutic properties, the resin has been employed to improve digestion and liver health.

The Aegean island of Chios is famed for the production of mastic resin and from the island the resin has taken its name, 'Tear of Chios', because, in common with all other resins, the gum mastic is released in droplets or 'tears'. In the 1st century AD Dioscorides reported that 'Chios mastic was sweet-smelling when white and clear and was chewed for a sweet breath.'

In the Bible, Daniel 13:54-55, is the story of Susanna, a fair Hebrew wife falsely accused by two lecherous voyeurs after they watch her bathing alone in a pool in her garden. The men accost her and threaten to report her for meeting a young man unless she makes love to them. Refusing this blackmail, she is arrested and about to be executed when Daniel uncovers a discrepancy concerning the tree under which the men claim Susanna met her lover. The first accuser declares it was a mastic tree, while the second says it was a holm oak; the obvious difference between the two trees proves the men were lying. The false accusers are put to death and virtue triumphs.

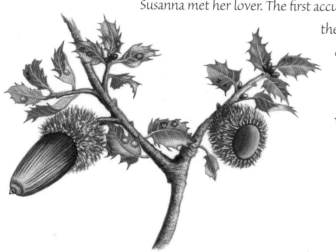

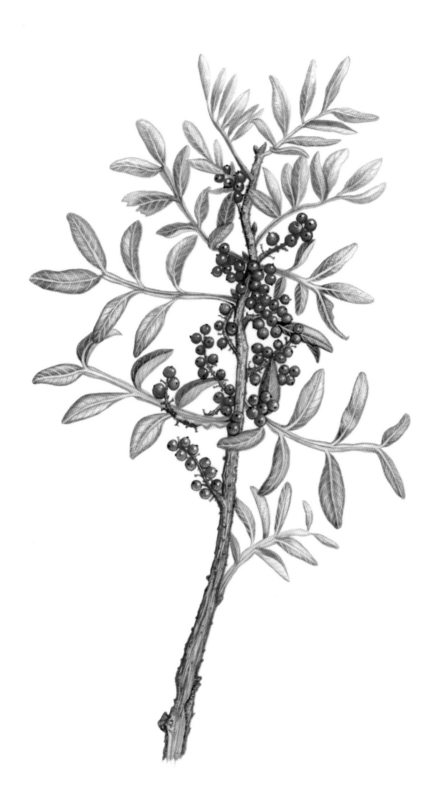

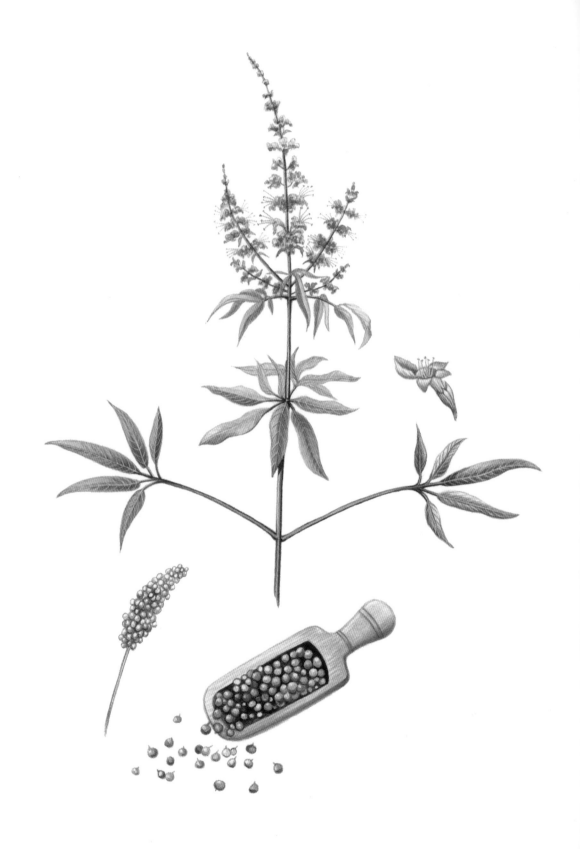

Chaste Tree or Monk's Pepper

Αγνή δέντρο

Vitex
agnus-castus

Swimming ashore to a deserted cove north of Antisami, Kefalonia, I strolled inland to investigate the flora and any fauna I might find. Bright green lizards scuttled out of my way to hide under rocks; the hypnotic, soporific humming of bees surrounded me as they sucked nectar from tiny wild thyme flowers, in sharp contrast to the shrill rasping of the cicadas.

The heat was intense beneath the rise; it wafted up in waves around me carrying with its earthy breath the aromatic scents of wild herbs and baked earth. A small tortoise dozed peacefully under a myrtle bush, looking as if his brown and cream patchwork shell had been recently polished. A large yellow butterfly fluttered in front of me, disturbed from its perch on a nearby flowering tree highly favoured by butterflies, the chaste tree or monk's pepper.

This grows on many Ionian islands, often around vineyards. As vectors, cicadas carry black wood disease to which grapevines are prone. Planted around vineyards as a biological control agent, monk's pepper is the only host tree for cicadas that efficiently contains them.

Monk's pepper was sacred to the virginal Greek goddess Hestia; the seeds were used in ancient Greece for thousands of years as an anaphrodisiac and given to men in holy orders to keep their minds and bodies free from lust. Theophrastus calls the tree *Agnos* (αγνός) meaning chaste.

In *Enquiry into Plants,* John Trevisa (1342–1402) of Trevassa, Cornwall wrote: '*The herbe agnus-castus is always grene, and the flore therof is namely callyd Agnus-Castus, for wyth smell and use it maketh men chaste as a lombe* (lamb)'.

In *Historia Naturalis,* Pliny the Elder describes Athenian women using monk's pepper leaves and stems as bedding to subdue passions during the *Thesmophoria,* when they left their husbands for three days each year to remain chaste. Whether the special bedding was required to pacify lonely husbands during the wives' absence, or by the women as well, remains a mystery.

Σταφυλίνακας   # Wild Carrot   Daucus carota

The humble wild carrot has an intoxicating aroma; its white root is the ancestor of today's modern carrot. Ancient Greek and Byzantine scholars wrote numerous reports on this plant. The root is rich in vitamins C, B, B2, iodine, sulphur, potassium, magnesium, iron and sugars. It is also rich in phosphorus, which may explain the belief that carrots help humans to see in the dark.

The dried flowers were used for kidney disorders and act as a potent diuretic. Infusions made from the seeds were used to treat colic pain and bloating of the abdomen. Dioscorides, the Greek physician and botanist who lived almost 2,000 years ago, wrote that the root could either be eaten after being cooked or soaked in wine for a few days. During the Minoan period, women ate wild carrots in the belief they would prevent obesity. In Cretan folk medicine it was recommended to drink a brew of seeds or the whole flower to treat kidney infections.

From March to April, before the plant flowers, fresh shoots are mixed with chicory, boiled and served with oil and vinegar. Its stem was once considered edible, although is no longer eaten. In more recent times it was discovered that the leaves of the plant have therapeutic properties, especially against carcinomas. These leaves are still being used in Cretan cuisine, in various dishes such as mixed braised greens and *kalitsounia*, small Cretan vegetarian pies. *Daucus carota* is often served in a mixture of *horta*: delicious wild greens boiled and served with olive oil and lemon juice.

Infusions made from wild carrot are used to treat coughs to this day. The plant was also used to predict rain: during March and April the plant was removed from the soil, hung out and left to wilt; before the rain, the leaves would revive again.

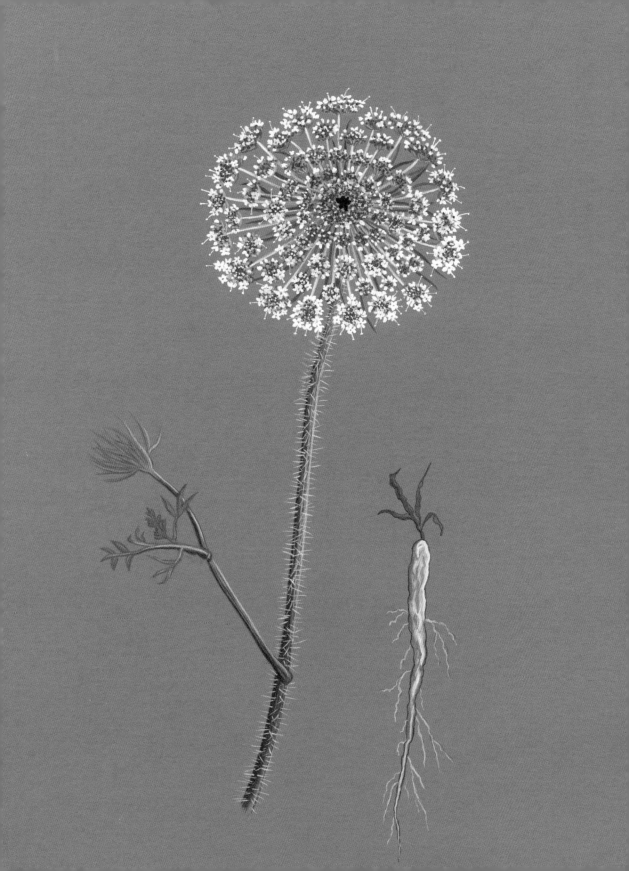

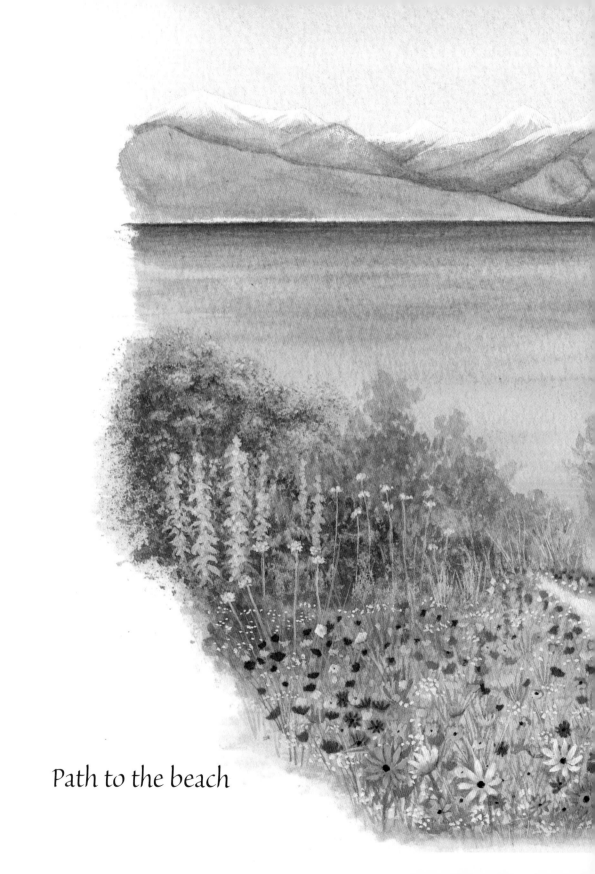

Path to the beach

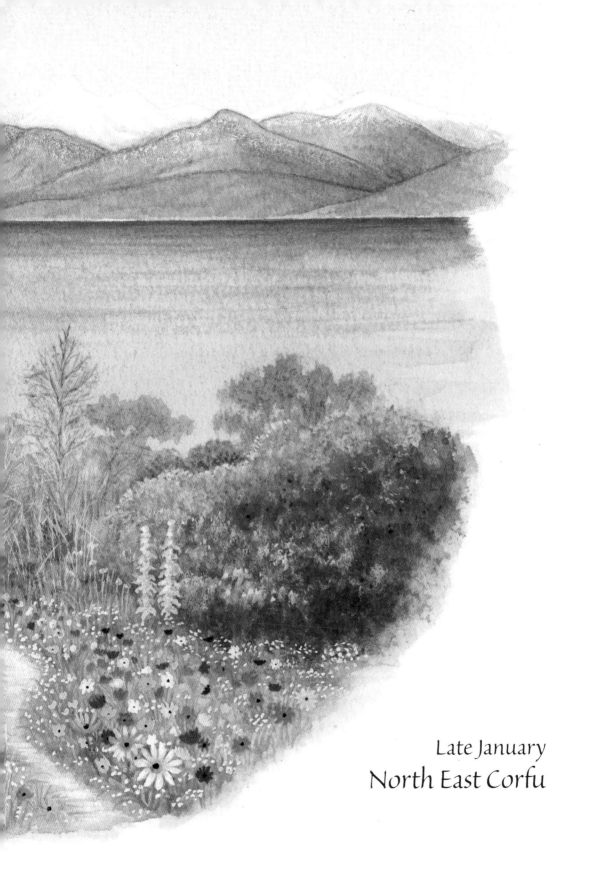

Late January
North East Corfu

Ανεμώνη   # Anemone   Anemone pavonina

Derived from the Greek *anemos*, meaning wind, the common name in Greece is windflower, because the delicate, papery flowers are blown open by the wind. In January the olive groves, fields, stony hillsides and pathways leading to the beaches of the Greek islands are spangled with anemones. From white to palest pink, magenta to wine red, they form a multicoloured carpet which heralds the arrival of spring.

In Greek mythology the beautiful goddess of love, Aphrodite, cried as she mourned for her lover Adonis, killed by the gods who were jealous of her love affair with him. According to legend, anemones sprung out of the ground where her tears fell.

In *Venus and Adonis* Shakespeare refers to the anemone:
   The field's chief flower, sweet above compare,
   Stain to all nymphs, more lovely than a man,
   More white and red than doves or roses are;
   Nature that made thee, with herself at strife,
   Saith that the world hath ending with thy life.

The anemone is used as an ingredient in perfumery; an example is the Italian scent Incanto, by I Profumi di Firenze.

Over fifty species of anemone have medicinal properties, some extracts and compounds having anti-inflammatory and antioxidant properties that are believed to be the forerunners of modern medicine.

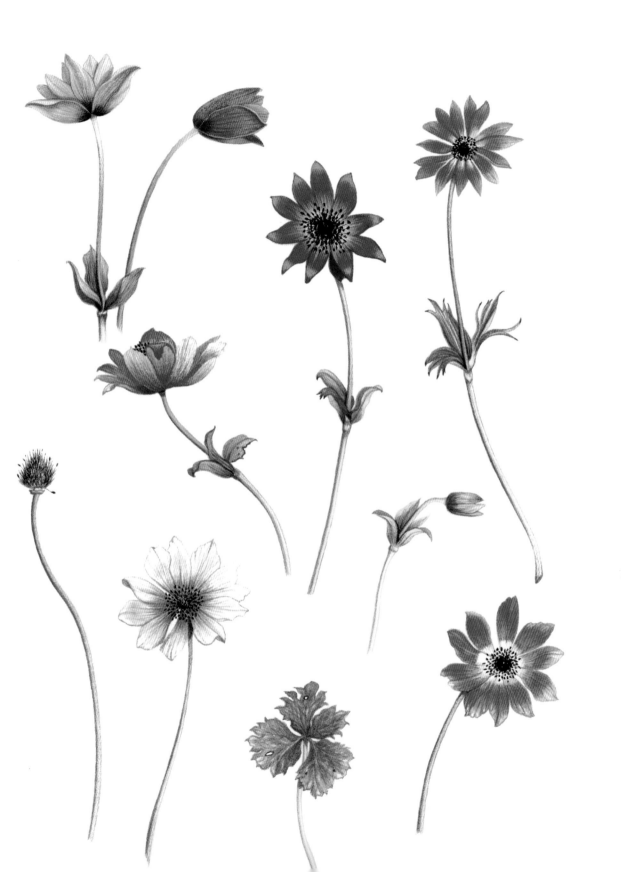

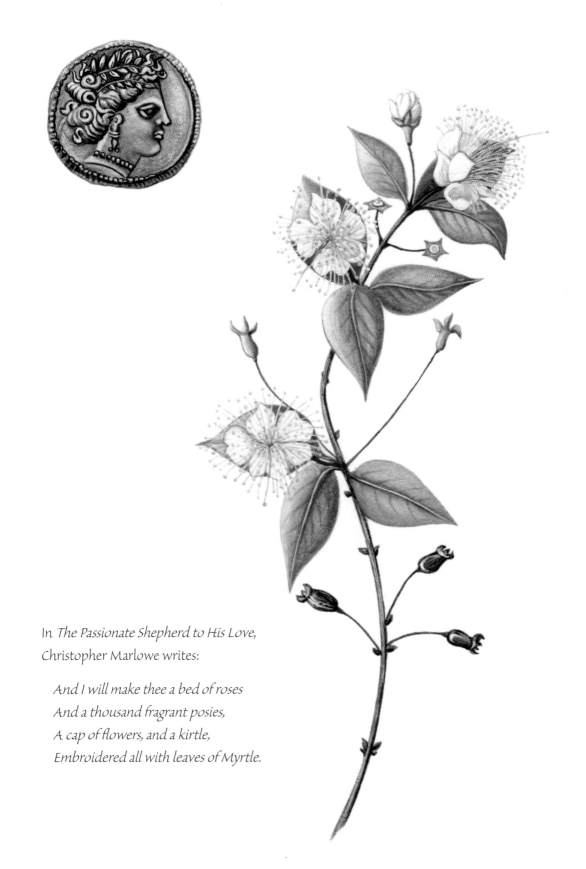

In *The Passionate Shepherd to His Love,*
Christopher Marlowe writes:

> And I will make thee a bed of roses
> And a thousand fragrant posies,
> A cap of flowers, and a kirtle,
> Embroidered all with leaves of Myrtle.

Μύρτος Myrtle *Myrtus communis*

In so many Greek Islands dense bushes of myrtle flourish on the littoral. On the tiny island of Anti Paxos, the delicate scent of myrtle flowers was carried from the land across the water to our catamaran on a raft of warm island breath.

In Greek mythology and ritual the myrtle was sacred to Aphrodite goddess of love and Demeter goddess of the harvest, who were often depicted wearing chaplets of myrtle.

Ονειροκριτικά, The Interpretation of Dreams

Artemidorus says that when interpreting dreams, *'A myrtle garland signifies the same as an olive garland, except that it is especially auspicious for farmers because of Demeter and for women because of Aphrodite, for the plant is sacred to both goddesses.'*

The myrtle plant was introduced to England in 1585 by Devonian Sir Walter Raleigh – a great favourite of Queen Elizabeth I. In 1858 Queen Victoria's daughter (also Victoria) had a sprig of myrtle in her wedding bouquet, from a bush presented to her mother. The flower of love, marriage and fertility, it has since become a tradition for British royal brides to carry a sprig of myrtle in their wedding bouquets; it is a popular addition to bridal flowers to this day.

Myrtle occupies a prominent place in the writings of Hippocrates, Pliny and Dioscorides. Prescribed for fever and pain by ancient physicians since at least 2500 BC, myrtle has high levels of salicylic acid, a compound related to aspirin.

In ancient Greece small black myrtle berries were eaten like nuts. Today many Mediterranean pork dishes include myrtle berries to add an aromatic flavour to the meat, the ground berries being used as a pepper substitute. The crushed leaves produce 'Eau d'Anges', an ingredient used in the production of perfume.

Insects

The Greek islands boast an enormous variety of fascinating insects, each having its unique and valuable place in the fragile ecosystem of its environment. However there are those who dislike sharing their favourite Greek haunts with these native creatures.

In John Mortimer's brilliant novel, *Summer's Lease,* a note is attached to the wall of the rental villa in Tuscany which has words of advice for its clients: *'Those alarmed by insect life should consider holidaying in Skegness'.* I copied this onto a small card for a friend who had built a stone-clad house high in the rocky hills above Kassiopi, which she let during the summer. She placed the card on the wall near the front door which, along with the French windows in the bedrooms, was always left open. The local insects found this most convenient, scuttling indoors at every available opportunity to enjoy the dual comforts of the shady rooms and cool smooth marble floors on hot days. The hills are a haven for wildlife of all sorts, including tortoises, lizards, snakes, rose beetles, scorpions, numerous species of butterfly and bee, hawkmoths, ladybirds, praying mantis and iridescent dragonflies. The abundant insect population surrounding the house had startled many visitors, although the children in the parties have been enthralled and kept entertained for the duration of their stay; as one parent commented in the visitors' book: 'We have never had such a peaceful holiday!'

Much to my friend's disgust, her expensive and carefully planted rose bushes fell prey to the outsized emerald green grasshoppers, whose favourite delicacies were rose petals. To my eyes these creatures were remarkable, looking like mechanical toys as their huge mandibles chomped away. With their triangular heads bobbing rhythmically up and down, they resembled the 'nodding donkeys' of the Texas oil fields. My friend had her own draconian solution to dispatching the insects. To my horror she chopped them in half with her secateurs.

Butterfly drinking dew on a tar globule

Bees nesting in a brick

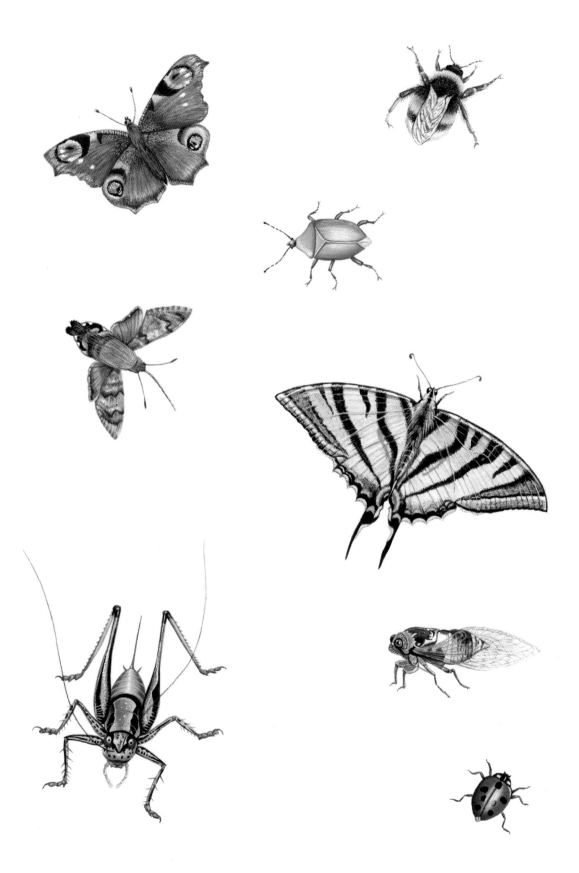

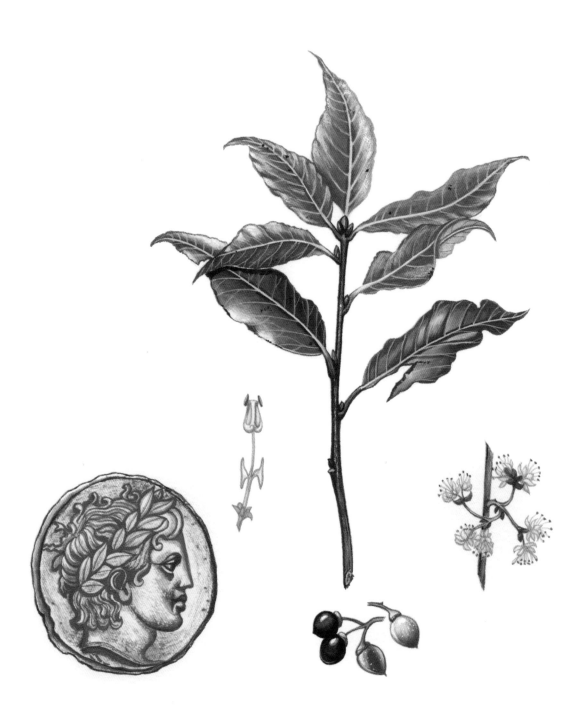

Δάφνη   # Bay   *Laurus nobilis*

Frequently mentioned in ancient Greek mythology, this evergreen tree symbolises courage and strength and was also treasured by the Roman gods, who wore sprigs of bay as crowns to represent their high status and glory. Greek myths also associate the bay with Apollo, this tree being one of his most important symbols. A wreath of bay was given as the prize at the Pythian Games, to honour him.

The ancient story of the bay tree begins with Apollo's pursuit of the beautiful nymph Daphne. She did not love Apollo so pleaded with her father, Peneus the river god, to turn her into a tree; according to the myth he turned her into a bay tree. Apollo decided that since he could not have his beloved Daphne as his wife, he would instead decorate himself with bay sprigs made from her branches.

The bay tree has glossy, evergreen leaves, which have been treasured for centuries for their aromatic quality. The leaves, which grow to a colossal size in Corfu, can be added to a bouquet garni or used alone to add a delicious flavour to soups and stews. In spring, the pale yellow blossoms attract butterflies and bees.

To this day, Greek housewives soak their white linen in a bowl of water containing handfuls of bay leaves to bleach the fabrics and rid them of stains.

Πυγολαμπίδα   # Fireflies   *Photuris pyralis*

One of the most magical sights I have ever seen is the pageant of fireflies on the islands at the beginning of summer. During the still May evenings soon after dark, beneath the olive trees, by streams and ponds or over any grassy patch, the dancing pin-pricks of neon yellow-green lights can be seen. Even a few feet from the lights of towns and villages, the fireflies will be found performing their mating ritual. There are over 136 species, each of which produces a unique pattern of flashes to attract the correct mate.

Although harmless, they contain the bioluminescent chemical luciferase, which helps to produce the light on their abdomen. This substance has been used in research into cancer, cystic fibrosis and heart disease. The colloquial name *kolofotios* translates literally as 'light-up bottom'.

I have held one in my hand and felt the vestige of warmth generated by its body. One night in May we found a swarm of fireflies illuminating the half-finished basement of the house we were building and considered the discovery most propitious.

I wish all early visitors to the Greek islands, especially those with children, would look for fireflies and marvel at one of the most enchanting sights in the natural world.

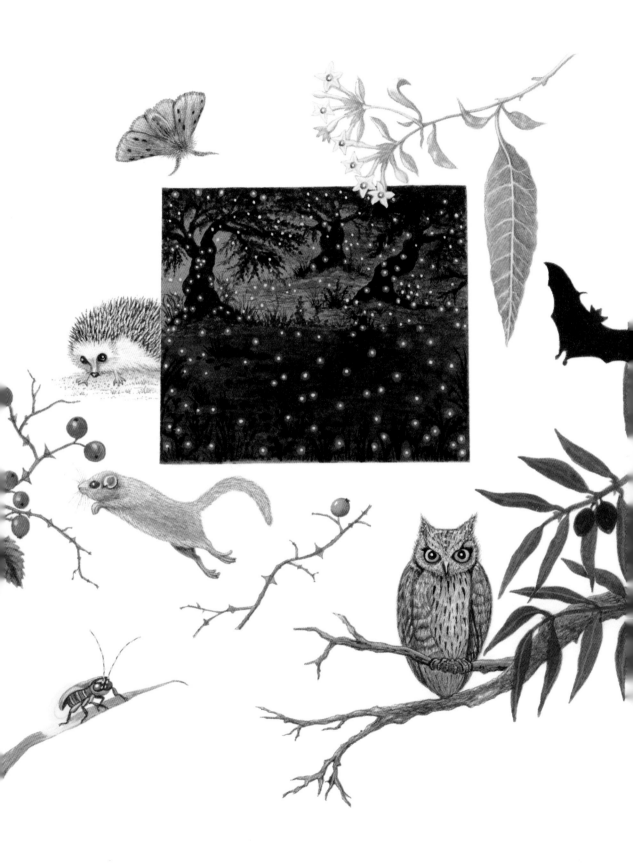

Edible Dormouse

One hot night when I was unable to sleep, I went outside the back door of our house above Kassiopi harbour to get some cooler air. Peering into the gloom, I heard the leaves of the plum tree rustling and noticed distinct and regular movements in the branches, although there was not a breath of wind. In August the branches were heavy with ripe fruit, some of which I had been able to pick: the dark purple plums were juicy and sweetly delicious. As I stared into the darkness, I could make out some little shapes creeping in the dense foliage, causing the leaves to shake with their movements. I could hardly believe my eyes, they were *glis glis* – edible dormice!

This name derives from the sad fact that the dormouse was farmed and eaten by the ancient Romans, Gauls and Etruscans as a snack, hence the description 'edible'. These sweet little furry nocturnal creatures with enchanting faces, large bead-like eyes and long fluffy tails were delicately plucking the plums and carrying them off stuffed in their mouths, presumably to feast on in the privacy and comfort of their homes. I wished my camera had been capable of capturing this extraordinary sight on film. Eventually, after half an hour or so, they scuttled off into the dark night and I never saw them again.

The next day I made some sketches of the dormice from memory and painted one leaping from branch to branch. The result was this painting, along with other nocturnal creatures to be found in the Greek islands, including fireflies and night-flowering plants. I found the tiny corpse of a horseshoe bat lying beside the pebble beach at Avlaki. In the freshwater lake behind the unspoilt beach I have also seen numerous terrapins, frogs, toads and wading birds. A lucky friend has also seen and photographed a pair of otters here.

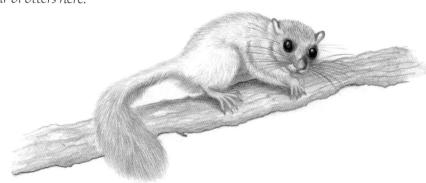

As darkness fell, it was fascinating to watch the local geckos from the front verandah of the house we lived in for several years whilst building our own home on the north east coast of Corfu. The property overlooked Kassiopi harbour and afforded uninterrupted views of the distant hills and mountains of Albania across the Corfu Straits.

Each night the geckos formed an orderly queue on the top of the streetlight at the bottom of our long flight of steps, waiting their turn in single file to catch moths as they circled the bright light. As soon as the front man had caught a moth, he would scamper past the queue with the moth stuffed in his mouth and disappear into the hole where the cable goes into the pole, presumably to eat his snack in private. Number two would do the same, and so on until, after the queue had all caught their prey, the first gecko would pop out of the hole, returning to repeat the process. The line was never broken until the first light appeared behind the mountains of Albania.

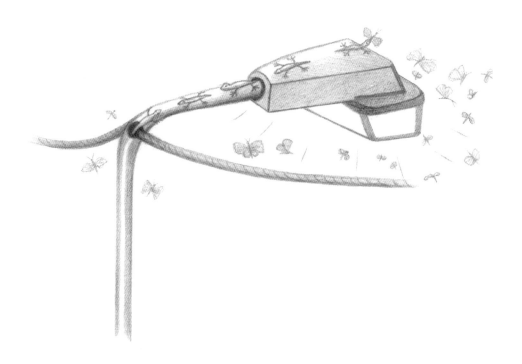

Dittany

Dittany of Crete, or hop marjoram, is a tender perennial plant that grows up to 30cm high. It is an extraordinarily powerful therapeutic and aromatic plant that can be found in the wild only on mountainsides and steep cliffs rising from the deep gorges of Crete. Its conservation status is officially 'Near Threatened'.

The leaves are teardrop-shaped, their downy white hairs giving them a soft velvety feel. When disturbed, the plant releases a pungent, spicy, oregano-like fragrance into the air; many people will smell dittany long before they see it. Indeed this was the case forty years ago when we took a motorbike up into the rugged mountains south of Chania, leaving our boat in the safety of the unspoilt Venetian harbour. I was lucky enough to be given a few sprigs by a shepherd and was able to study them closely.

Believed to be a magical plant, dittany was used in making potions; it is even mentioned in the *Harry Potter* stories, when 'Essence of Dittany' is used to heal a snake bite.

Pliny the Elder stated that deer consume dittany to expel arrowheads from their wounds – a story that is part of Greek folklore. Much later Jeremy Taylor (1613–1667), the English cleric and writer of poetic prose, wrote of the male red deer:

The hart wounded with an arrow runs to the herb dittany to bite it, that the shaft may fall out that stuck in his body.

Symbolising love, dittany is held to be an aphrodisiac. Yet only the most ardent young lovers scaled the mountainsides of Crete to gather bunches of the pink flowers to give as love tokens; over the centuries numerous would-be Romeos and Casanovas have fallen to their deaths as they attempted to gather the herb. In recent times commercial collectors of dittany are known as *Erondades* – Love Seekers.

Drinks flavoured with dittany include vermouth and absinthe.

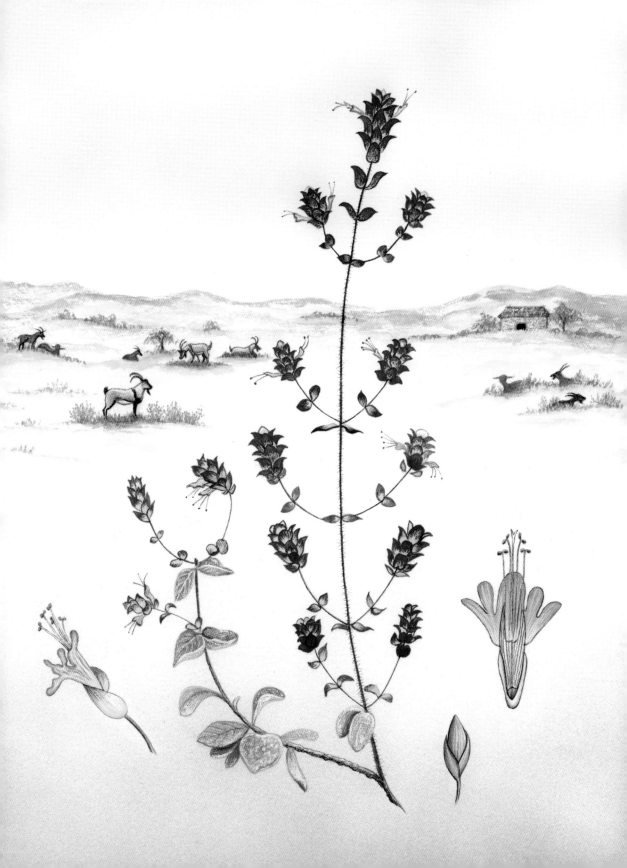

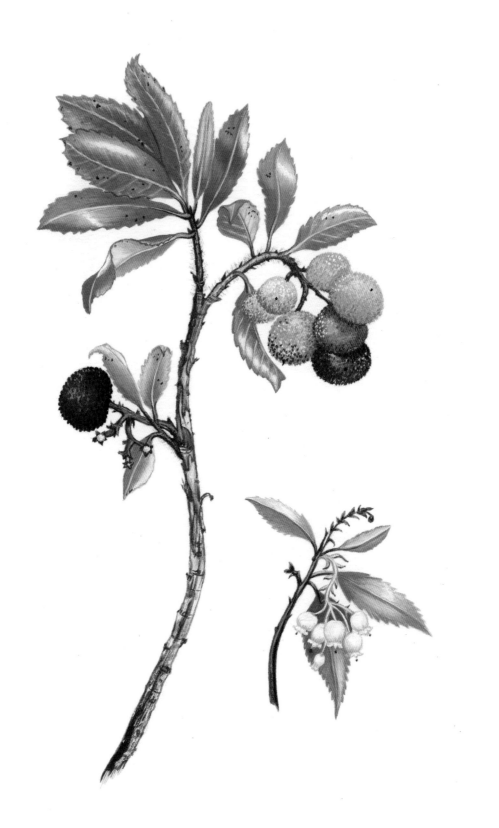

Strawberry Tree

The hermaphrodite flowers appear in autumn on this profuse tree alongside the fruit, which is edible but strangely bland for such an attractive and prolific crop. As such, summer visitors to the islands will never see the arbutus tree in its full glory, dressed all over with white flowers and clusters of large berries varying between yellow and red as they ripen.

The name unedo may have been coined by Pliny the Elder, being a possible corruption of *unum edo*, or 'I eat one' (and only one), referring to its distinct lack of flavour.

The brown and grey bark of more mature trees peels back naturally to reveal an attractive, raw sienna-coloured skin beneath; as such, the stems of arbutus are often used for decoration.

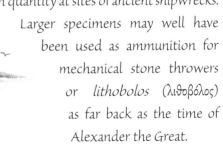

High in the hills above Agios Stefanos, at the rim of a well in the shade of a mature arbutus, I found this fossilised sponge. I refer to it thus without any idea of the correct name, which is suggested only by what I have been told, as well as its shape, texture and the noticeable imprint of a stem.

Abundant in the Ionian, these fossils vary from marble to football size; they can often be seen protruding from sedimentary rock faces exposed by erosion or earthworks. Intriguingly they have also been found in quantity at sites of ancient shipwrecks.

Larger specimens may well have been used as ammunition for mechanical stone throwers or *lithobolos* (λιθοβόλος) as far back as the time of Alexander the Great.

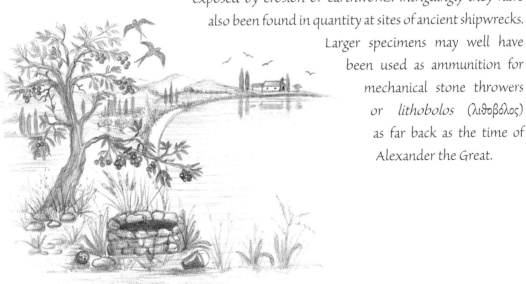

White Flowers and Shells

In mythology, the Greek goddess of flowers is Khloris (or Chloris), wife of Zephyrus, god of the West Wind. Khloris was associated with spring, the beginning of new life in the plant world. In his beautifully intricate painting, *Primavera*, (The Birth of Spring) Sandro Botticelli portrays Khloris next to her Roman equivalent, the goddess Flora.

White flowers have always been my favourite; jasmine, gardenia, lily-of-the-valley, frangipani, narcissus, and stephanotis. Unsurprisingly, knowing my love of scent, they all have wonderful perfumes. I gathered white flowers from the verges lining the path to the white pebble cove where I swam at dawn each morning when we were at anchor in Kassiopi Harbour. Butterflies were everywhere, flitting around aromatic camomile daisies and dainty Star of Bethlehem flowers. I decided to paint a picture of white flowers when I returned to Sarava, with a cabbage white butterfly and a pearly white shell I had found on a remote beach in Ithaca. The ancient Greek for butterfly is psyche, meaning soul; Psyche was also the name of the human lover of Eros. I had discovered some subtly coloured craft card in Corfu Town, perfect for these delicate white images which would not show well on white paper.

Dainty white sand crocus carpeted a patch of short grass above the beach, filling the warm air with the unmistakeable aroma of currant buns. Eventually I discovered the reason – the three long deep red stigmas of the sand crocus's relation, *Crocus sativus*, are laboriously gathered by hand to make saffron, a key ingredient for flavouring the buns. The stigmas of sand crocus are not gathered but obviously the deliciously sweet scent produced is the same in both species.

The most valuable spice by weight, saffron is also a powerful antioxidant. Originating in Greece, saffron was revered for its medicinal properties. Greeks would eat saffron to enhance libido, boost mood and improve memory.

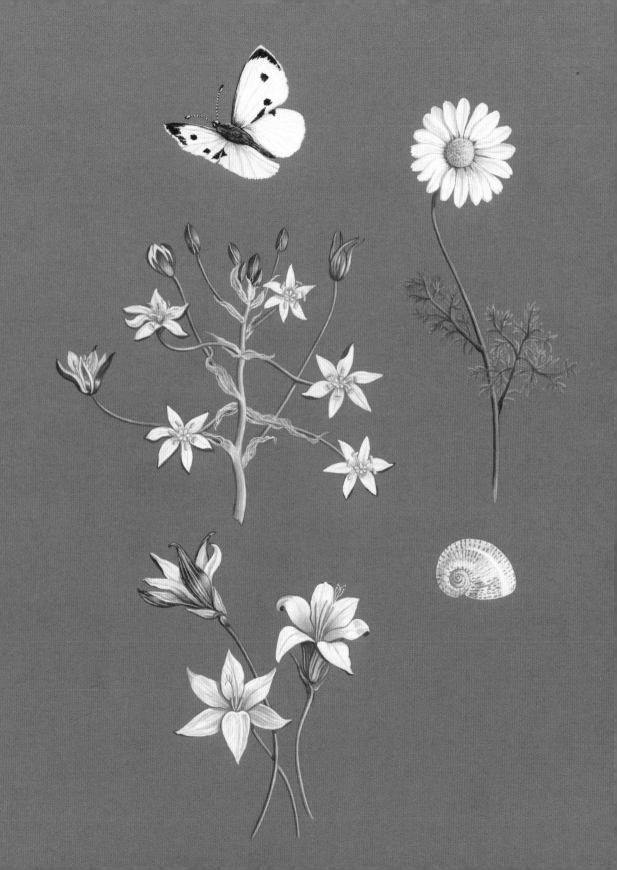

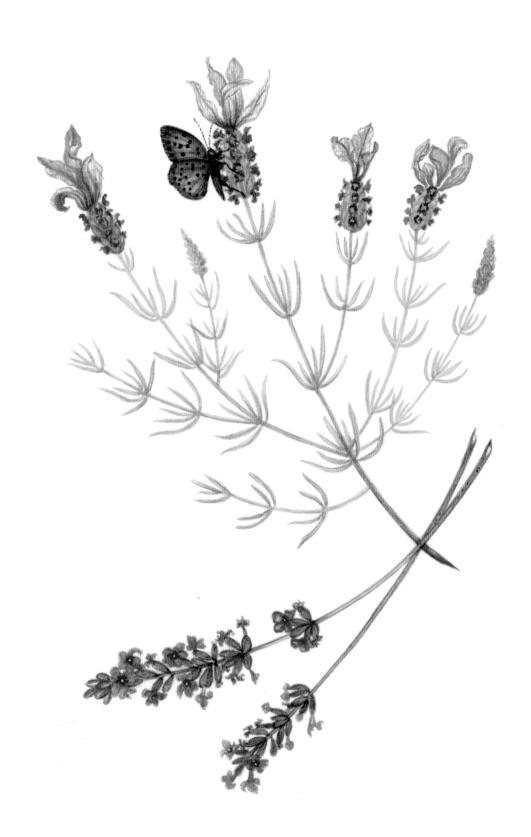

Lavender

In summer when the islands were full of lavender I picked bunches, hanging them inside our catamaran to dry. Removing the stalks from the dried flowers, I filled small muslin bags with the blossoms. I put them in all the cupboards and lockers, not only keeping moths away but making everything smell clean and fresh, no matter how long it was stowed.

Ancient Greeks called lavender 'Spikenard' or 'Nardus' after the city of Naarda. The English word is derived from the Latin *lavare*, to wash, due to lavender's cleansing properties. Lavender has an anti-inflammatory as well as a calming and soothing effect on skin, body and mind. I am always delighted to see sprigs of rosemary or lavender used to brush olive oil on spit-roasting lambs, thus infusing the meat with their flavour.

Lavender Shortbread

160 gr plain flour
100 gr unsalted butter
Pinch sea salt

75 gr caster sugar
1 egg yolk
1 teaspoon good vanilla extract

1-2 teaspoons dried lavender flowers

Mix all ingredients except egg yolk until it resembles fine breadcrumbs. Add egg yolk and form a soft dough. Roll dough to 1cm thick. Using a wine glass, cut out biscuits. Place on a baking tray lined with greaseproof paper. Bake at 170°c for 8-10 minutes. When golden, remove from oven and cool on a wire rack.

Attach a few crystallised lavender flowers on each biscuit with a spot of wet icing. To crystallise flowers, paint thoroughly with egg white, sprinkle with caster sugar and leave to dry for two days.

Panacotta with Kumquat Sauce

450 gr fresh milk	150 gr caster sugar
600 gr double cream	7 sheets of gelatine

Put cream, milk and sugar into pan and bring to the boil, stirring continuously. As soon as mixture reaches boiling point, remove from heat. Immediately add gelatine sheets (previously soaked in warm water and squeezed out) and stir until melted. Leave to cool and pour into glasses. Cool in fridge for at least 5 hours.

Syrup – Mix kumquat liqueur with finely chopped kumquats, crystallised or fresh. Drizzle syrup over panacotta when ready to serve.

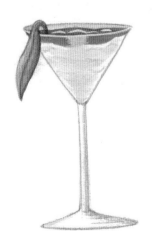

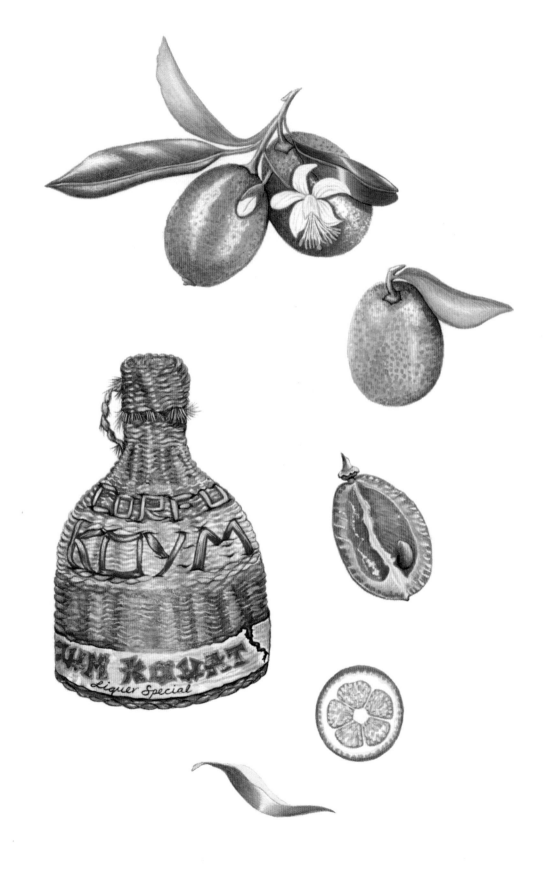

PAINT COLOURS

I have always been enchanted by the names of different paints and their origins; raw sienna, viridian, burnt umber, vermilion, indigo, quinacridone gold, cerulean blue, magenta. The semi-precious stone lapis lazuli was ground to a fine powder to make ultramarine, the most expensive of all blue pigments; the name derives from Middle Latin ultramarinus, literally 'beyond the sea' because it was imported

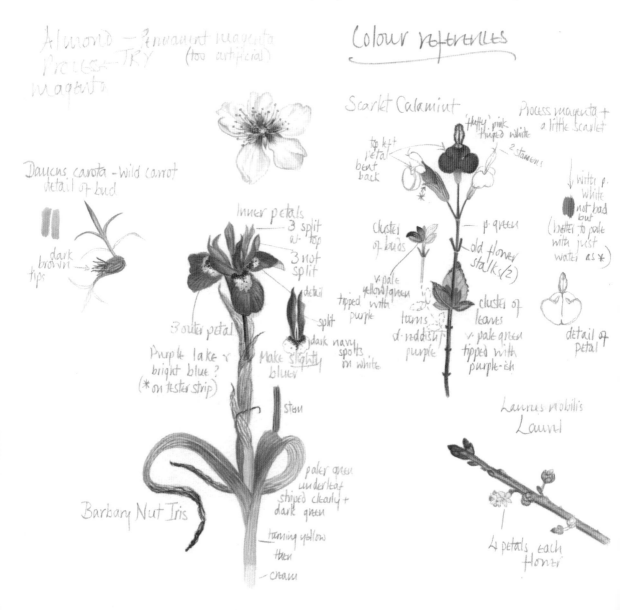

Almond — Permanent magenta
Process—TRY   (too artificial)
magenta

Colour references

Scarlet Calamint

'fluffy' pink
tinged white

top left
petal
bent
back

2 stamens

Process magenta +
a little scarlet

Daucus carota - Wild carrot
detail of bud

dark
brown
tips

with p.
white
not bad
but
(better to pale
with just
water as *)

Inner petals
3 split
w. top
3 not
split

cluster
of buds

p. green

old flower
stalks (2)

v. pale
yellow/green
tipped with
purple

turns
d. reddish
purple

cluster of
leaves
v. pale green
tipped with
purple-ish

detail
detail of
petal

split

3 outer petal

dark navy
spots
in white

Purple lake r
bright blue?
(* on tester strip)

Make slightly
bluer

Laurus nobilis
Laurel

stem

Barbary Nut Iris

paler green
underleaf
striped clearly +
dark green

turning yellow
then
cream

4 petals each
flower

by sea from Asia. A metamorphic rock, lapis has been prized since antiquity for its intense deep blue colour. During the seventh millennium BC lapis lazuli was extracted from the Sar-i-Sang mines in northern Afghanistan.

The stone was used in the fabulous funeral mask of Tutankhamun, which I was lucky enough to see at the Tutankhamun Exhibition at the British Museum in 1972. In Bhirrana, India, lapis lazuli artifacts have been found dating to 7570 BC; lapis beads have been found in Mauritania. By the end of the Middle Ages lapis lazuli was exported to Europe, where it was made into ultramarine. The leading artists of the Rennaissance and Baroque periods, including Titian and Vermeer, used ultramarine, although it was often reserved for the clothing of the central figures of their paintings, especially the Virgin Mary.

Biological pigments were often difficult to obtain and their manufacturers kept details of their production secret. Tyrian purple is a pigment derived from the mucus of the murex shell. It was greatly valued as a dye for fabric and used by the Phoenicians as early as 1200 BC; the Greeks and Romans continued production until the fall of Constantinople in AD 1453. The pigment was complex and expensive to produce; consequently items coloured with the dye were symbols of wealth and power. Julius Caesar was often portrayed wearing a robe of 'royal purple', while the members of his Senate wore white robes decorated with a single stripe of purple signifying their inferior status.

List of Species

Scarce swallowtail	Ποδαλείριος	Podalirius
Olive	Ελιά	Olea europaea
Pomegranate	Ρόδι	Punica granatum
+ Emperor dragonfly	Λιβελούλα	Anax imperator
Sea Daffodil	Κρίνος της θάλασσας	Pancratium maritimum
+ Lily borer caterpillar	Χάμπ	Brythis crini
Honeysuckle	Αιγόκλημα	Lonicera etrusca
+ Oleander hawk moth	Σκώρος γερακιών	Daphnis nerii
Snake's Head Iris	Ίριδα η κονδυλόριζη	Hermodactylus tuberosus
Caper	Κάππαρη	Capparis spinosa
+ Seahorse	Ιππόκαμπος	Hippocampus
Hoopoe	Τσαλαπετεινός	Upupa epops
Shells	Κοχύλια	Concha

Species pictured: Euspira catena, Tonna galea, Trunculariopsis trunculus, Opercula, Lutraria oblonga, Hexaplex trunculus, Monodonta adriatica, Cardioidea, Venus verrucosa, Haliotis tuberculata, Solecurtus strigillatus.

Jasmine	Γιασεμί	Jasminium polyanthum
Mediterranean Poppy	Παπαρούνα	Papaver
Lemon Tree	Λεμονιά	Citrus
Kingfisher	Αλκυόνη	Alcedo atthis

Species pictured: Glaucium flavum, Capparis spinosa, Posidonia oceanica, Euspira catena, Hippocampus, Hexaplex trunculus, Paracentrotus lividus, Tamarix aphylla, Alcedo atthis, Anax imperator, Lampides boeticus, Lonicera periclymenum, Gonepteryx rhamni, Calystegia soldanella, Jasminium polyanthum

Species pictured on spread 2: Malcomia littorea, Lycopsis arvensis, Paracentrotus lividus, Cardium echinata, Luria lurida, Solecurtus strigillatus

Common Sandpiper	Ακτίτης	Actitis hypoleucos
Papyrus	Πάπυρος	Cyperus papyrus
Passion Flower	Λουλούδι του πάθους	Passiflora caerulea
Snowdrop	Γάλανθος	Galanthus reginae-olgae
Convolvulus	Περιστροφή	Convolvulaceae
Calamint	Καλαμίνθη	Clinopodium nepeta
Wild Pea	Λάθυρος	Lathyrus clymenum
European Chipmunk	Ταμίας	Eutamias sibiricus
Cyclamen	Κυκλάμινο	Cyclamen persicum
+ Pink hawksbeard (left)	Κρεπίς η ερυθρή	Crepis rubra
+ Field scabious (right)	Κναούτια η αρουραία	Knautia arvensis

Nuts and Seeds	Καρπούς, σπόρους	Nuces, semina

Species pictured: Eucalyptus globulus, Melia azederach, Quercus coccifera, Quercus ilex, Juglans regia, P hybrida, Cercis siliquastrum, Schinus molle, Aesculus hippocastanum, Quercus cerris, Cupressus sempervirens, Paliurus spina-christi, Prunus amygdalus, Acer monspessulanum, Castanea sativa.

+ Rose chafer beetle	Κρυσοσκανθαρος	Cetonia aurata
Narcissus	Νάρκισσος	Narcissus tazetta
Mastic Tree	Μαστίχα	Pistacia lentiscus
+ Kermes oak	Πουρνάρι	Quercus coccifera
Chaste Tree	Αγνή δέντρο	Vitex agnus-castus

+ Bees: Bombus lapidarius (top), Xylocopa violacea (middle), Bombus terrestris (bottom)

Wild Carrot	Σταφυλίνακας	Daucus carota
Anemone	Ανεμώνη	Anemone pavonina
Myrtle	Μύρτος	Myrtus communis
Insects	Έντομα	Insecta

Species pictured: Aglais io, Bombus terrestris, Palomena prasina, Papilio machaon, Cicadoidia, Coccinella septempunctata, Eupholidoptera chabrieri, Macroglossum stellatarum.

Bay	Δάφνη	Laurus nobilis

+ Bees: Apis mellifica (top), Bombus terrestris (bottom)

Fireflies	Πυγολαμπίδα	Photuris pyralis

Species pictured: Diaphora mendica, Cestrum parqui, Rhinophus ferrumequinum, Otus scops, Photuris pyralis, Glis glis, Erinaceus europaeus. Lavandula stoechas.

Edible Dormouse	Μυωξός	Glis glis
Gecko	Γκέκο	Hemidactylus turcicus
Dittany	Δίκταμο	Origanum dictamnus
Strawberry Tree	Κουμαριά	Arbutus unedo
White Flowers		

Species pictured: Pieris napi linnaeus, Anthemis arvensis, Euspira catena, Romulea bulbocodium, Ornithogalum umbellatum.

Papillon Lavender	Λεβάντα	Lavandula stoechus
True Lavender	Λεβάντα	Lavandula angustifolia
+ Purple-edged copper butterfly	Λυκαίνα Ιππόθοης	Lycaena hippothoe
Kumquat	Κουμκουάτ	Citrus japonica
Balkan Green Lizard	Τρανόσαυρα	Lacerate trilineala

Multiple species are listed clockwise from top left.

Please note, this is not a scientific text book — merely the diary of an enthusiastic amateur naturalist. Some English, Greek or Latin names may not reflect or identify exact sub-species, but I have done my best!

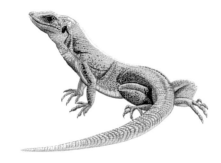

Nature creates nothing without a purpose.

Aristotle

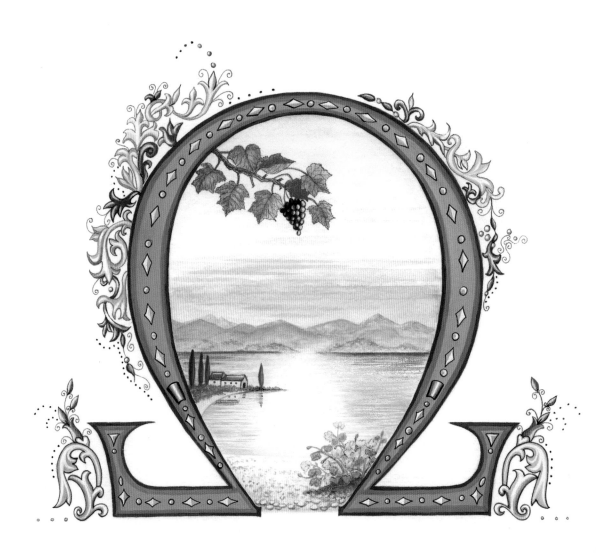

After women, flowers are the most
lovely thing God has given the world.

Christian Dior

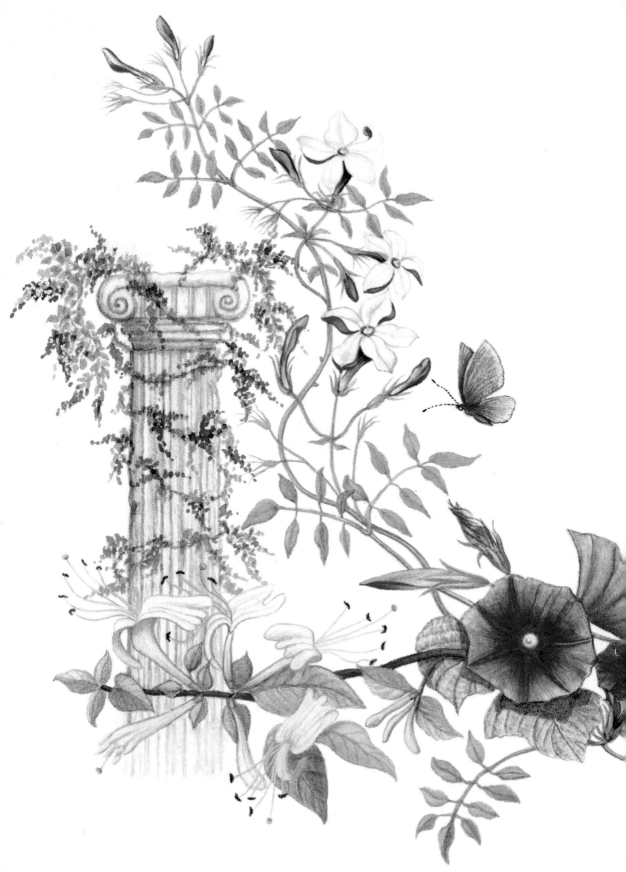